All the Way to Lincoln Way

A COAST TO COAST BICYCLE ODYSSEY

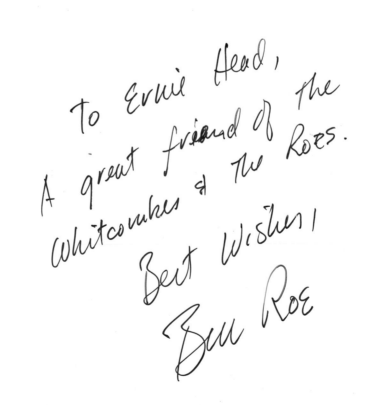

To Ernie Head,
A great friend of the
Whitcombes & The Roes.
Best Wishes!
Bill Roe

Bill Roe

ROWHOUSE
PUBLISHING
Davis, California

All the Way to Lincoln Way
A COAST TO COAST BICYCLE ODYSSEY

Printed in South Korea
ISBN: 0-9703188-0-4

Book and cover design
Alison Roe • Modern Art

All photographs by Bill Roe
(except as noted)

Cover Photos
Photo of Bill by Eric Roe.
Photos of Golden Gate and
Brooklyn Bridges by Bill Roe.

FIRST EDITION

ROWHOUSE
PUBLISHING

3500 Anderson Road
Davis CA 95616
bilroe@aol.com

C O N T E N T S

When the spirits are low, when the day appears dark,
when work becomes monotonous, when hope hardly seems worth
having, just mount a bicycle and go out for a spin down the road,
without thought on anything but the ride you are taking.

—Arthur Conan Doyle

PROLOGUE

Carl Fisher was a man with ideas. He took a strip of swamp land at the southern end of the Florida peninsula and created Miami Beach, one of our nation's most successful real estate developments and popular tourist destinations. Earlier in his life, Carl was a bicycle racer and a bike salesman. He later broke a couple of auto racing world records and raced against Barney Oldfield, one of the most famous early race car drivers. His idea for the Indianapolis Speedway was born from this interest in automobile racing. The Indianapolis 500 supplied a proving ground for the fledgling auto industry, a place to develop faster and more reliable cars.

In 1912, Carl Fisher had another big idea, an improved highway that would run from the Atlantic Ocean all the way to the Pacific. At first, he called it the "Coast-to-Coast Rock Highway," but Henry Joy, the president of Packard Motor Car Company and one of the businessmen who put up the seed money for the project, suggested that the new highway be named for Abraham Lincoln. Ultimately, the road left Times Square in New York City, crossed the Hudson River into New Jersey and then continued west through Pennsylvania, Ohio, Indiana, Illinois, Iowa, Nebraska, Wyoming, Utah, Nevada and California, all the way to Lincoln Park in San Francisco.

Today the great Lincoln Highway only exists in frontage roads, isolated country lanes and in dozens of small towns along their main streets – many of them still called Lincoln Way. Much of it has been paved over by interstate highways, but older residents along its length remember when the Lincoln Highway brought the world to their front doors. In my mind it still connects the places that mean the most to me: San Francisco, my favorite city in the world; Davis, California, my home town; Iowa, where I grew up and went to college; New York City, where my daughter now lives.

So it made sense, at least to me, to travel these old roads following the Lincoln Highway as closely as possible. Americans had followed parts of this same trail on foot or horseback, in covered wagons and in Model Ts. My idea was to travel the same route on my Trek UAV bicycle – 3,300 miles in eight weeks.

When a traveller returneth home,
let him not leave the countries
where he hath travelled
altogether behind him.

—Francis Bacon

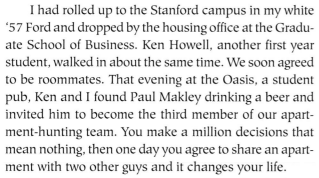

I didn't wake up one morning and decide to ride my bike from San Francisco to New York City. Strange as it sounds, I would have to trace the beginnings of my 1999 bike trip back to Palo Alto, California and a fateful September day in 1965.

I had rolled up to the Stanford campus in my white '57 Ford and dropped by the housing office at the Graduate School of Business. Ken Howell, another first year student, walked in about the same time. We soon agreed to be roommates. That evening at the Oasis, a student pub, Ken and I found Paul Makley drinking a beer and invited him to become the third member of our apartment-hunting team. You make a million decisions that mean nothing, then one day you agree to share an apartment with two other guys and it changes your life.

Ken had the most important role to play: he introduced me to his girlfriend, Nancy Whitcombe. When Ken and Nancy broke up, Nancy and I began dating. We fell in love and were married in 1968, returning to her hometown of Davis, California, one of our nation's premier bicycle towns. I joined her brother John building custom houses. A few months later Paul Makley, my old roommate, joined our company and the three of us have been partners for nearly thirty years.

Was it destiny that brought us all together? I have often wondered how different my life would have been had Ken and I not arrived at the housing office at the same time. I also wonder if I would have decided to ride a bike across the country if I had ended up living in Houston, for instance.

At first, Nancy was not convinced that the bike trip was a good idea. But, she finally agreed to come along, learning to drive the twenty-four foot motor home that carried our gear, serving as both a "sag wagon" and our home. She decided that my chances of surviving a 3,300 mile odyssey were improved if I didn't have to attempt it alone. Her support – both practical and emotional – was critical throughout the entire trip. She rode to my rescue many times, saving me from hail storms, lightning, flat tires, and slumping spirits.

Thanks, Nancy. The journey would not have been complete without you.

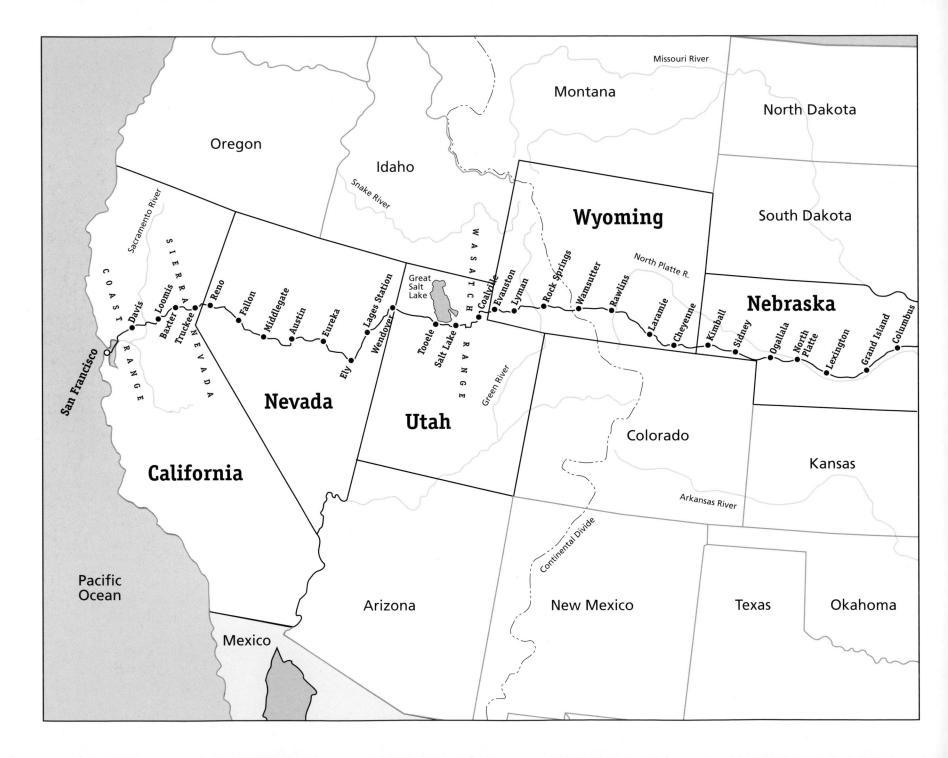

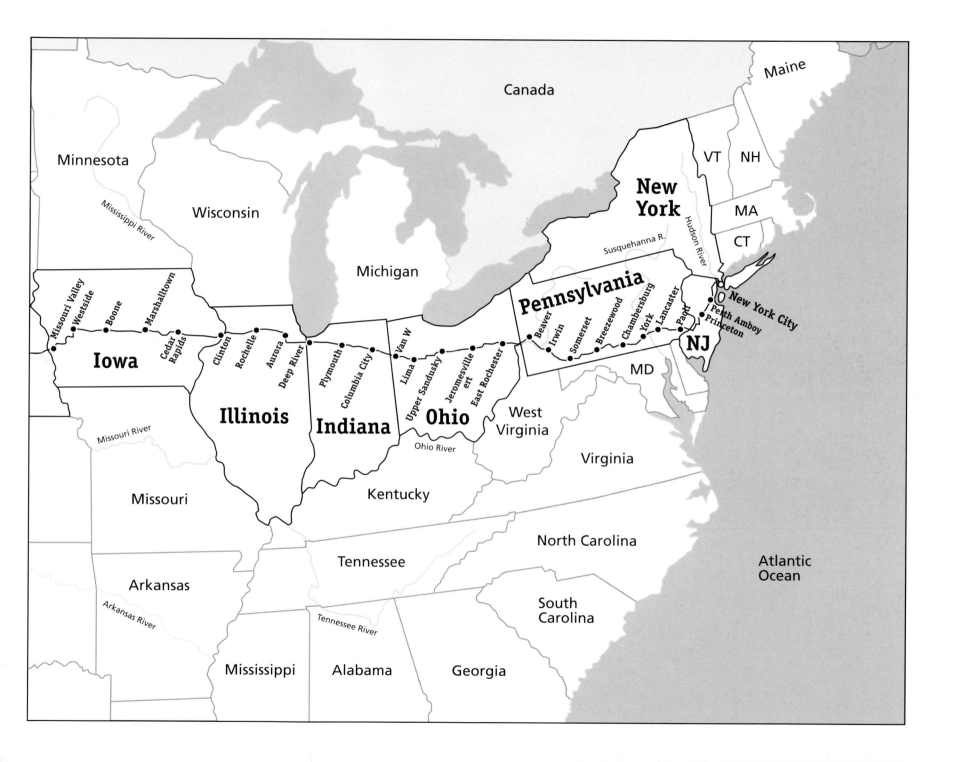

Only that traveling is good which reveals to me the value of home, and enables me to enjoy it better.

—Henry David Thoreau

CHAPTER ONE
California

May 27 - Day 1
San Francisco
The Beginning

The dark gray Pacific Ocean extended to the horizon as far as we could see, flat and uninviting, under a dull gray sky. It was cold when I stepped out of the car and I reached into the back seat to grab something warmer, a long sleeved jersey to pull on over my cycling shirt. The weather was warm, maybe even hot, when we had left Davis and California's Central Valley an hour and a half earlier. Here at the coast the temperature was in the low fifties.

I unloaded my bike and pushed it towards the water, across a hundred yards of absolutely deserted beach – the landmark Cliff House restaurant looming above me to the north. The water was freezing and the wind was cold. I had visualized this day a hundred times. There was always a flaming sunset, dramatic colors reflecting in a sparkling sea. I would dip the rear wheel of my bike into the Pacific, with my finger pointing triumphantly eastward. Presently, I couldn't even see the sun through the thick layer of fog streaming in towards the city. I decided it was now or never. I reached into the ocean and filled a small glass bottle I planned

to carry with me across twelve states and empty into the harbor at the end of Manhattan Island. I stood in the surf, barefoot, preoccupied, worried that my gears were being damaged by the salt water, waiting for Nancy to finish taking pictures with her camera, my camera and our video. "Patience," I thought, and tried to ignore my numb feet.

I pushed my bike out of the ocean and across the wide stretch of beach, the wet wheels picking up more and more sand. Salt water and sand are bad medicine for bicycles, so I picked up my bike and lugged it the last seventy-five yards across the beach and up the stairs to the top of the sea wall. The bike's tires and my feet, both encrusted with sand, created a pressing minor emergency, solved with the sacrifice of some bottled

Above left: Bill begins his journey in San Francisco, dipping his wheel in the Pacific – the Cliff House looming behind.
Above: An anique post card with an earlier view of the Cliff House, circa 1915.
Facing page: The Golden Gate Bridge, the symbol of San Francisco.

Post card views of the 1915 Panama-Pacific Exposition (top) and the Ferry Building with the Bay Bridge in the background.

May 28 - Day 2
San Francisco to Davis
74.6 miles

San Francisco was still fogged in the next morning, but it didn't seem as cold and windy as the day before. Nancy and I had breakfast at Mel's Drive-In on Lombard before I left for the Ferry Building and my trip across the bay to Vallejo. Breakfast in a drive-in seemed the perfect way to begin following the historic Lincoln Highway. I hoped to find and photograph many of the older diners, gas stations and motels as I rode across the country. I wasn't optimistic, however, that the photos of the city I hoped to take this morning were going to be very good. There wasn't any sun and the Golden Gate was nearly invisible in the distance, almost hidden by the fog. I rode past a series of San Francisco landmarks. Marina Green had plenty of joggers and bike riders, despite the cool summer weather. Fisherman's Wharf was quiet, the tourists not yet surrounding the stands selling crab cocktails. Soon I could see the familiar profile of the San Francisco-Oakland Bay Bridge, completed in 1936, marching west from Yerba Buena Island. "Yerba Buena," or "good herb" in Spanish, was the city's original name. In 1837, when the city had a population of 500 people, the name was changed to San Francisco by proclamation.

I arrived about twenty-five minutes early at the Ferry Building, its tall, square tower anchoring the foot of Market Street, and found 150 eighth graders waiting to go with me. They were celebrating their graduation with a trip to Marine World for the day.

The kids didn't distract me too much from the sports page. I did glance up at the world-famous skyline of the city through windows obscured by spray. Alcatraz Island and the bridges grew smaller as we raced away on

water Nancy had in the car. I put on my socks and cycling shoes and, dressed and shivering, I was finally ready to start my journey to the Atlantic. My head ached. It was not an auspicious beginning.

I rode up the hill past the Cliff House, climbing steadily. The effort both warmed me and helped soothe my anxiety that our commencement was somehow flawed. I met Nancy about mile away in Lincoln Park, the official western terminus of the Lincoln Highway. On several beautiful San Francisco days I had admired the view of the Golden Gate Bridge from this spot. Not now. We could hardly see beyond the trees that lined the golf course. I had hoped to ride across the bridge this afternoon and take some pictures, but quickly decided I would have to return another time. We dutifully recorded our presence in the growing afternoon dimness and set out through the Presidio for the Palace of Fine Arts. This building is the only remaining fragment from the grand Panama-Pacific Exposition of 1915 celebrating the opening of the Panama Canal. The event was one of the motivating forces to create a transcontinental highway – a highway that would allow people to drive an automobile from the Atlantic to the Pacific. What an adventure!

our twin hulls. I had selected the perfect city, my favorite place on earth, for the beginning of my journey, but had chosen a day that left much to be desired. When we arrived in Vallejo about an hour later, the sun was out.

I remembered the first time that I rode my bike to the Vallejo ferry terminal, on my way into San Francisco. I boarded in the early afternoon with two other cyclists. Both of their bikes were heavily loaded, with their front and rear wheels carrying double panniers or saddle bags. Sleeping bags and other equipment were piled on over the handle bars. The bikes were being propelled by a small, slender English woman and her French boyfriend, both in their late twenties. It was hard to believe that she could make that heavy bicycle move forward on flat ground, let alone up a significant incline.

All three of us sat on the lower deck of the ferry to be near our bikes. I was curious about their trip and asked, "How long have you two been on the road?"

"We started in Alaska a couple months ago," the woman answered. "Amazing," I thought, but when I asked about their ultimate destination, I was shocked.

"Tierra del Fuego in Argentina," she replied. Remembering that encounter, I felt that my plans to ride across the United States seemed almost sensible.

The idea of a cross-country ride evolved over the last eighteen months as I explored routes, times and other logistics. I purchased books of maps to study, quizzed Bicycle Coordinators in twelve states, and searched the Internet for advice from bike club members across the nation. Finally, I chose a route that I hoped would be safe and interesting – traveling west to east to take advantage of prevailing winds. I selected a time that I expected would miss the snows in the mountains and the worst of the heat in the deserts.

I rode away from the harbor and started over the coastal range outside of Vallejo – a warm-up for the Si-

erra Nevada mountains that lay ahead. As I neared Cordelia, I noticed in my rear view mirror an older, faded, blue-green Lincoln approaching me from behind. It didn't seem to be traveling fast and I paid no attention to it until the front fender suddenly appeared next to me, only a foot to my left. Before I could turn away or even think anything else, I felt a sharp slap on my left buttock and heard a loud whoop. Then, right in front of me, I saw a young girl – long blond hair flapping wildly in the wind – crawling back through the rear window of the car while laughter and screams drifted out. The en-

The ferry from San Franciso at the Vallejo pier with Bill's bike leaning on the rail in the foreground.

tire upper half of her body had been dangling out into space. I smiled, waved and guessed that this was my first experience with those car/bike conflicts I had been warned about. If this was as bad as it was going to get, I wasn't going to worry about it – I might even look forward to it.

After Cordelia, I followed the old road north to

Rockville and then east into Fairfield. At the end of Main Street, I passed the courthouse and stopped to admire the Lincoln Highway marker that remains out front. On September 1, 1928, Boy Scouts across the country marked the highway with concrete posts, averaging about one per mile. They installed nearly 3,000 of them, two of which remain in my hometown of Davis. A small bronze disk with a bust of Abraham Lincoln is imbedded in the pillar. Around his profile are the words, "This highway dedicated to Abraham Lincoln." These posts were the last act of the original Lincoln Highway Association. It was re-activated in 1992, dedicated to preserving the highway.

Pleasants Valley Road, one of the most beautiful places to ride in the Sacramento Valley.

North Texas Street was several miles of strip malls and fast food. I made good time through the stop lights and was soon out of town into the hills.

I stopped just west of Vacaville to visit the old Vaca-Peña Adobe, one of the first homes in this part of the state. The building wasn't open but I took a break in the surrounding park, imagining what it was like to be an early settler in this region. The Vaca and Peña families left Sante Fe for California in 1841. They registered as immigrants with Mexican authorities at Pueblo de Los Angeles and continued north where they successfully petitioned for a Mexican land grant of ten leagues of grazing land. Here in the lovely Laguna Valley they established their home. They raised cattle, producing tallow and hides, and lived a prosperous existence until the Bear Flag Revolt forced Mexico to give up claims to California. Squatters and other claimants gradually eroded control of their ranch. The Vaca and the Peña families continued to live in the area, leasing land they had once owned.

Just across I-80 from the adobe is one of the better remaining remnants of the original Lincoln Highway. The tree-lined road curves gently back and forth and crosses a bridge built in 1912. This narrow two-lane road is little changed from the time when it carried open touring cars across the country – a road dominated by the landscape, where pavement followed the land forms and avoided the farmlands.

I turned off the old highway onto Pleasants Valley Road, one of the most beautiful cycling roads in the Sacramento Valley. It is tucked between two ranges of rolling hills. The grass was just beginning to change from winter green to summer yellow, or "California gold." The western side of the valley easily rose high enough to earn the name "mountain." From a distance, these mountains, covered with knolls, knobs and promontories, resembled a pile of blankets, heaped on an unmade bed, rumpled and folded, hiding a sleeping giant.

The air was fresh, the traffic almost nonexistent. Solitary old oak trees dotted the sloping pastures. Groves of eucalyptus, rows of palms, and weathered, tin roofed barns stood near the road. White painted wooden fences framed the views. The oak trees spread over and above the road creating shady tunnels to ride through. The valley began to narrow – almost a canyon. I crossed a bridge over a stream that appeared in the constricted end of the valley. The road crossed back and forth over the stream, as though the builder had trouble making up his mind which side of the valley provided the best route. In this area, I recently startled two vultures feeding on a dead deer lying only a few feet off the side of the road. They were ugly and large enough to cause me some concern about my own safety. This spring I startled a flock of wild turkeys after I came around a bend.

I was hungry, anxious to reach Winters for lunch at my favorite cafe. Riding east on Putah Creek Road, I reached up into an overhanging tree and grabbed a handful of ripe cherries. They tasted so good, I decided to buy some more. I turned up a driveway to a stand in the farm yard. The orchard country around Winters is always a wonderful place to ride. In the spring, when the trees are full of blossoms, it's amazing. In 1842, John R. Wolfskill arrived in this region with fruit seeds and cuttings and became the father of the area's fruit industry.

Putah Creek Cafe is a favorite stop for bike riders in this orchard country – great food and friendly service. On weekends you almost always see several bikes parked out in front. But on this Friday afternoon, I had the place entirely to myself. I looked out the window. Across the street from the cafe, a Mexican fan palm soared over four stories above the ground. A sign next to it read, "PLANTED, in 1902 by, D. O. JUDY."

After lunch, I headed back along Putah Creek to Davis with only fifteen miles to go – another wonderful bike road. I left the hills behind and rode out onto absolutely flat land. For the next forty miles I would travel through an area that in ancient times was the bottom of an inland sea. I rode through peach, apricot and almond orchards, the trees planted in perfect rank and file – even the diagonals were flawless. Long rows of aged olive trees lined the road in several places – the gnarled, twisted trunks looking like the weathered faces of old men.

After crossing the graffiti-covered, but still beautiful, arched Stevenson Bridge over Putah Creek, I turned onto the Russell Boulevard bike path for the five mile trip into Davis. The magpies were thick, hopping on fences out of my way, and then gliding gracefully into the fields, their black and white formal attire looking like tuxedos leaving a dance. Bright yellow beaks and subtle neon turquoise on their tails provided contrasts with their traditional dress.

At Cactus Corner, I rejoined the Lincoln Highway and followed it into town under a row of walnut trees. This western entrance to Davis is distinguished by this avenue of giant, old trees, a noteworthy landmark on the Lincoln Highway. These walnut trees, many with trunks over six feet in diameter, were planted in the 1870s and have sheltered drivers from the hot summer sun for over a century. I rode into town, the University of California at Davis on my right, and turned up Anderson Road, happy to have my home just a mile away.

The ancient oak trees, planted in the 1870s, along Russell Boulevard in Davis.

May 29 - Day 3
Davis to Loomis
65.2 miles

The day started well enough with the temperature in the low sixties. I rode back to the University, returning to the Lincoln Highway. This University of California campus, one of nine, was established in 1905 to provide agricultural training for Berkeley students on a university farm. Today it is an independent campus with 25,000 students pursuing degrees in everything from agriculture and art to law and veterinary medicine. The students comprise nearly half of the population of the city. Davis claims to be the second most educated city in the nation after Chapel Hill, North Carolina and has been a pioneer in bicycle transportation, with 50 miles of bike paths connecting all sections of

Top: A crowd gathers every Saturday at the Davis Farmers Market.
Center: A post card view of the Yolo Causeway between Davis and Sacramento, taken about 1919.
Bottom: A West Sacramento motel on Capitol Avenue, the old Lincoln Highway.

the city. Twenty-five percent of all daily trips are made by bicycle, the highest percentage in the country. It's known as "The City of Bicycles" and has more bikes per capita than any other city in the nation.

My neighbor, Bob Brouhard, is fifty-four and a real Davis "bike nut." He began biking seriously about six years ago. His first major ride was the Davis Double Century, an annual two hundred mile ride held every May. He left Davis with twelve hundred other fanatic cyclists at five in the morning and returned, much the worse for wear, just before ten at night. But he made it. Bob spent the spring and summer of 1999 training for the Paris-Brest-Paris bike race in August, one of amateur cycling's premiere events. He completed the 760 mile course in a little over eighty hours. That's nearly 200 miles a day, four days in a row. He admitted that he didn't sleep much. Now, does that sound like an entertaining European vacation?

In 1999, every member of the Davis Bike Club was invited to ride either 500, 1,000 or 1,500 miles during the month of March – an event called "March Madness." I rode exactly 1,003 miles during the month, considered it training for my upcoming cross-country ride, and was pleased with myself. Bob more than doubled my total and only came in fourth. His buddy Larry Burdick, who is sixty years old, won the event, riding 3,720 miles, an average of about 120 miles a day. Bob described the day, late in the month, when Larry rode up to his house and asked for help zipping up his jacket. His hands had turned into claws, so stiff from holding onto the handlebars they were unable to grip the small end of the zipper. Larry is another genuine Davis bike nut. Living in a town like Davis near people like Bob and Larry certainly provided me with the necessary inspiration to contemplate a cross-country ride.

The Davis Farmers Market in Central Park was in full swing when I rode by. Another of the 1928 Lincoln Highway markers was located on the northwest corner of the park. I stopped to take a picture of the 1917 railroad underpass and an old motor court a block to the east on Olive Drive. The motor court had a variety of small cabins connected by flat roofed carports that would be a little small for a modern sport utility vehicle. It was well preserved, primarily because the motel units had been resurrected as rentals; funky, affordable abodes for students. I headed east on an old piece of Highway 40 that had been turned into a bike path, Interstate 80 to my right and the transcontinental railroad to my left. I would travel alongside these two major thoroughfares most of the way to New York City.[1]

For three miles across the causeway the bike path runs adjacent to the freeway. The road noise is unpleasant, but the beauty of the wetlands to the north always makes the journey interesting. I saw several white egrets wading in the shallow waters. Standing, they appeared almost frail, with long necks and legs and a small oval shaped body. It amazed me when they took flight, two huge wings magically appearing from nowhere, giving the birds size and power, moving gracefully, ghostly white spirits soaring across the marsh. In the winter the causeway fills with water, recreating that vast inland sea that once occupied California's Central Valley. The valley is one of the richest farm regions in the world – America's Salad Bowl. But the route to Sacramento was too familiar; I had made the run so many times. I was still finding it difficult to believe that I was on a cross-country journey.

In West Sacramento, West Capital Avenue is home to dozens of motels, thousands of rooms. All of them have seen better days – the days when the Lincoln Highway and US Highway 40 poured thousands of potential customers along the avenue past these businesses. The grand El Rancho, once one of Sacramento's finest hotels, is now called "The City of Darma Realm." It is home to a religious sect and has barbed wire strung around the top of its old stucco walls. Motels have been renamed to attract a new clientele. The Dude Motel competes with Experience Lodge/The Adult Motel for business. Signs advertised rooms available by the week or the month.

After crossing the Tower Bridge over the Sacramento River, I found the Memorial Day weekend Jazz Festival just getting underway. As I rode into Old Sacramento and could hear the music from the outdoor venues, I regretted missing one of my favorite events. Bands come

At right: An old post card view of the Tower Bridge in Sacramento. Below: A statue of a rider celebrates the end of the Pony Express Trail in Old Sacramento.

[1] *I elected to ride across California while living at home. The four-day trial run over Memorial Day weekend gave me a chance to test my conditioning while gaining some confidence. It also included a major challenge – the Sierra Nevada Mountains and Donner Summit at 7,240 feet. A three-day recovery period followed this experiment before I resumed the journey – complete with loaded motor home – at the California-Nevada border. The first four days included many comings and goings, as I rode progressively further away from home. I was retrieved by Nancy at the end of each day and returned the next morning to the same spot.*

The American River bike path, a beautiful, shady place to ride.

from all over the world. The festival has expanded from its Dixieland roots to include big band, jazz and blues.

I stopped to take a picture of the statue of the pony express rider, a reminder that I would also be following that trail across parts of Nevada, Utah, Wyoming and Nebraska. Sacramento was the western terminus of the Pony Express. A copy of President Lincoln's first address to Congress in March of 1861 reached Sacramento from St. Joseph in only seven days and seventeen hours, the fastest run ever between the two cities, averaging 255 miles per day. The transcontinental telegraph was completed on October 24, 1861, and the Pony Express closed officially only two days later, eighteen and half months after it opened. The freight company of Russell, Majors and Waddell, that financed the operation, lost over $100,000 during the wild romantic ride.

The Railroad Museum had a locomotive on the massive turntable out in back as I rode by. Steam was exploding out of it in all directions, creating a ball-shaped cloud of white smoke, fifty feet in diameter. Since the Lincoln Highway and the railroad are nearly constant companions on their journeys across the country, I visited this museum a few months ago while preparing for my ride. Inside there is a dining car with a collection of china and silver from the various rail lines across the nation. The star of the show is the *Governor Stanford*, the first locomotive of the Central Pacific Railroad. A wicked looking cow catcher projects to the front, a huge smokestack points toward the sky and yellow brass provides bright decoration along its entire length. It was shipped around Cape Horn and arrived on the Sacramento waterfront in 1863. It was soon put to work, helping build the transcontinental railroad, just a few feet from where it currently stands.

I followed the Sacramento River north for a mile and turned onto the American River bike path. It was beautiful and busy with weekend joggers and riders, the green of new leaves everywhere, marshes full of water and vines climbing the trees.

I labored along, tiring rapidly, running out of fuel. The last five miles were difficult, but I finally reached Folsom around noon. My normal cereal-and-banana breakfast hadn't been sufficient to last fifty miles. I "bonked," the cyclists' term for running out of energy. I also didn't drink enough fluids. My right leg and hip began to ache. How was I going to make it to Truckee by Monday night, let alone manage to ride sixty miles a day for seven more weeks? At this point, I didn't know.

In Folsom, I went directly into a restaurant, drank a huge glass of iced tea, and then started on a pitcher of water that was left on my table. After the tea and the water I began to feel a little better. My food arrived and I consumed it ravenously. It seemed as if I had been fasting for days. I had to do a more intelligent job of eating and drinking or I'd never see New York City.

After lunch I rested and walked around town, waiting for my strength to return. By the time I set off for Folsom Dam, and the road across the top of it, I had recovered. Three miles later, I arrived at the dam only to learn that bikes were prohibited. I had no choice; I had to return to Folsom and cross the American River there in order to head north to Loomis, my destination for the day. Not a perfect day so far, but I only had eighteen miles to go.

As I rode away from the river I began to climb. I was no longer riding through the flatlands of the Sacramento Valley or along the banks of the American River. I was on my way over the foothills of the Sierra Nevadas. It was harder work, but I was enjoying it more. It made a difference traveling a road I hadn't ridden before. There were even occasional downhills. The doubts and frustrations of a few hours ago began to vanish – a day at a time, a mile at a time.

May 30 - Day 4
Loomis to Baxter
46.7 miles

Back in Davis, I was up early and quietly sneaked out of our bedroom, trying not to wake Nancy. After I dressed and ate some breakfast, I loaded my bike into the trunk of the car and headed back to Loomis. Sacramento and Roseville rolled by and a little less than an hour later, I was unloading my bike. Despite the relatively brief time in the car, it seemed an impressive distance from home, a long way to travel on a bike. The old road to Newcastle climbed steadily, meandering past old roadhouses and the historic Griffith Quarry. The quarry, established in 1864, supplied stone to major projects in Sacramento and the Bay Area. A small building constructed out of the handsome gray stone with the characteristic sparkle of granite sat beside the road. I walked back to the quarry and looked down into the huge pit cut out of solid stone, its lower depths filled with water. It was easy to see how it could have supplied materials for hundreds of large structures.

Old motels along the road looked like a series of

connected cottages, now converted into apartments. In Newcastle, the old fruit packing sheds with rusty metal roofs were deserted, waiting to be converted into restaurants and stores. I left town, crossed under the railroad and turned toward Auburn. Anyway, I thought I had turned toward Auburn. I started downhill, slowly at first, and then, as the slope became steeper, more swiftly. It had to be a mistake; there was way too much downhill. I was headed in the wrong direction and stopped as quickly as I could. Discouraged, I struggled back up the steep incline I had conquered only a few minutes earlier. It was bad enough the first time, but to do it again, with so much climbing still remaining over the next two days, was a case of insult to injury.

When I finally reached Auburn, I stopped to photograph a 15-foot statue of a miner panning for gold, standing at the entrance to the historic downtown. Auburn was one of the important gold rush towns of 1849. I stopped for a drink and a snack at a store with a friendly Chinese proprietor who remembered back in the forties when the Lincoln Highway ran through town right by his store. The old-fashioned general store was dim towards the rear, away from the front windows that supplied the best light. The owner's clothing was clean, neat and well preserved and looked like it had been purchased in the '60s. Both the store and the owner had a weathered charm, a true synergistic relationship, creat-

Above: A 15-foot miner pans for gold in Auburn with the railroad and I-80 in the background.
Below: Bill stands before a vibrant mural in downtown Loomis.

Above: The Placer County Courthose rises above Lincoln Way, Auburn's main street. Below: A dilapidated roadside lodge east of Colfax.

ing a special feeling inside the old building. It was a place that would have suffered with remodeling. Refreshed, I started back up Lincoln Way, past the old courthouse. "Up" was the right word and it would be an accurate way to describe my route for the rest of the day. The road to Colfax followed I-80 and the railroad, crossing under or over each of them several times, creating a braid of concrete, steel rails and asphalt. Conifers gradually began to replace the deciduous trees and the temperature dropped a bit as the elevation increased.

Another steep, but thankfully short, climb and I crossed I-80 one more time before riding down into Colfax. The downtown is spread out along the north side of the railroad, across the street from the depot. This railroad town was created in 1864 when the transcontinental railroad was being constructed and is still an important rail yard. I was ready for lunch, about halfway into a fifty mile day, and stopped at a little cafe. It was a popular place and no tables were available. I sat down at the counter next to a guy, about sixty, who confirmed my choice of cafes.

"This is the best place in town. I try to come here for lunch a couple times a week." He was retired and lived up the road about ten miles out of town. When I told him what I was doing, he informed me that I had a "short uphill" after Rollins Lake, and that the road on the way to Applegate wasn't too bad. "Good," I thought.

Just east of town I rode past an old roadside lodge. Only the stone foundation was left from the main building, but a circular row of cabins remained. Some of them were still occupied while others were beginning to fall into disrepair. Each one had a river rock fireplace and a metal Quonset hut style roof. I wondered what this complex would have looked like when it was new and how long ago that would have been.

Following the old highway, I had a pleasant run

downhill to Rollins Lake where the weekend was in full swing with boats on the lake and bathers on the shore. I started up again right away, shifting down into my lowest set of gears. It was steep and I was soon breathing hard, my mouth wide open, attempting to gather as much air into my lungs as possible. Deep breaths rushed noisily into and out of my body. My luncheon partner had said a "short uphill" so I struggled on, confident I would soon reach the crest. It was slow going. I traveled less that two miles during the next twenty minutes. I began to feel, almost hear, my pulse throbbing in my head, beating like a trip hammer. This was the warning bell that my body wouldn't stand much more of this nonsense. I stopped and had a drink, waiting for my overworked heart to drop below 100 beats per minute.

It was a pretty road; I hadn't noticed with my head down and my mind focused on my pedals. The road curved as it climbed, rocky cliffs to my left and a pine forest to my right, with a swift-moving creek running through it. Back on the bike I continued up the hill, hoping to reach the end of this agony. Finally I rode out of the forest and stopped on a freeway overpass, resting, watching the traffic flow by below me. If that was a short uphill, I wasn't looking forward to a long one.

The road through Applegate was beautiful and, thankfully, didn't have as much climbing. I was starting to tire and I knew I still had over an hour of riding. I called Nancy and made arrangements for her to pick me up at Baxter. I passed the rusted residue of an old gas station with a single gas pump, standing like a sentinel along the road. I crossed the freeway once again and followed the railroad into Dutch Flat – at various times a wonderful old mining, railroad and Lincoln Highway town. It's not much of anything today. A cafe sits on one side of the road next to an old boarded up hotel, and the general store in a stone building on the other

side. The store has been in business since 1854. A sign, hanging over the door listed all ten people who had owned the building, up until the present day. The safe in the building arrived by mule train in 1860. I had a drink and pulled off my shoes, allowing my aching feet to recover. I wasn't able to do as much for my sore butt, except remove it from the bike seat for a spell.

Three miles later I reached Baxter, not a town, but a freeway exit with a gas station and a restaurant. Both were closed, out of business permanently it appeared. I sat in the shade, drinking the rest of my water, waiting for Nancy who arrived fifteen minutes later. I was tired and glad that I only had one more day of climbing in order to reach the top of the Sierra Nevadas at Donner Summit. I groaned as I crawled into the car. Nancy dropped me off in Loomis and I drove back to Davis.

June 1 - Day 5
Baxter to Truckee
39.1 miles

After breakfast, we drove back into the mountains to the Baxter exit. At the end of the day, I planned to get off my bike for three days and attempt to recover from this trip across California. I needed the break to heal my aching body and prepare for the trip. I had Tuesday through Friday noon to finish up projects at work and complete packing the motor home with supplies for the twelve weeks we would be gone. I didn't have to remember everything; forgotten items would certainly be available in Reno, Salt Lake or some other place east of there. Weighing more heavily on my mind were concerns about whether I could survive the nine or ten days in a row of biking across Nevada and the Great Salt Lake Desert into Salt Lake.

The decaying remains of an old gas station near Applegate.

Left: The railroad and I-80 with the snow-capped Sierra Nevada in the distance. Right: The turbulent south fork of the Yuba River near Rainbow Lodge.

After Baxter, my first seventeen miles were on the Interstate and that was unpleasant enough – noisy, large trucks and buses racing by just ten feet away. That wasn't my biggest problem, however. The road was climbing steadily for as far as I could see. I kept thinking that up around the next bend it would level off. It didn't and the first seven miles took me almost an hour. There was a fairly constant six or seven per cent grade, so I was climbing about 350 feet every mile – over 2,000 feet in that first hour. Beyond the first summit, I rode out of the trees; the majestic snow-covered crests of the Sierra appeared before me with the road winding endlessly into the distance. It was only thirty miles from where I stood to Donner Summit, but my eyes and tired body said, "It looks a lot farther than that."

I arrived at Cisco Grove and exited the Interstate. Hallelujah! In all fairness, at least three of those seven-

teen miles were downhill, but the balance of the journey was a grind. It helped to be somewhat unaware of the obstacle I was facing. I found myself refusing to look at the road vanishing upward into the distance. It became too discouraging. I forced myself to ride at least another tenth of a mile before I peeked, hoping to see the crest, praying for a level stretch of road.

I stopped at the gas station for a candy bar and a large iced tea. Back on my bike, I felt better – the sugar helped and the road was not climbing as rapidly. I was riding, virtually alone, on an old two lane highway surrounded by forest, the freeway noise barely audible to the south. Small picturesque stone and log cabins were set along the road back in the trees. Several overlooked the Yuba River that followed the road for long stretches. A lone rock fireplace signaled the location of a cabin that had burned to the ground. At eleven-fifteen, I pulled into Rainbow Lodge, a lovely old inn.

I'd always wanted to eat here, but never found the opportunity. I felt a little strange sitting at a linen covered table dressed in my cycling gear, but the food was so good I soon forgot my attire. This must have been a pleasant watering hole on the old highway. It still is. The inn overlooks a tranquil pool where the river slows momentarily before continuing its rush down the mountain. After lunch I stretched out in an Adirondack chair under some trees by the pond for about fifteen minutes.

Fortified, I began my assault on the summit and the road immediately forced me into lower gears. The south fork of the Yuba River roared by, only a few feet from the road. This spring, an impossible amount of water was forcing its way through a series of giant boulders, creating a turbulent whitewater landscape. Almost none of the blues and greens associated with the color of water were present. The sun created rainbows in the mist produced by the hundreds of waterfalls. The crashing turmoil was both marvelous and frightening, a perfect companion for a ride through the mountains.

"The snow is melting into music..." is how the naturalist John Muir described a similar Sierra stream in his journal, *My First Summer in the Sierras*. He wrote of a beautiful spring day in 1869. "*Another glorious Sierra day in which one seems to be dissolved and absorbed and sent pulsing onward we know not where. Life seems neither long nor short, and we take no more heed to save time or make haste than do the trees and stars. This is true freedom, a good practical sort of immortality...*" It was my wish to experience this "true freedom" on our trip.

The combination of a tired body and a continuously rising road made the next fifteen miles difficult. The scenery helped, but it couldn't push the pedals. I could see drifts of snow under the trees away from the road. Just before the top, I passed Sugarbowl and Soda Springs

A beautiful spring day at Donner Lake.

ski areas and then a high meadow with a freight train heading down the valley toward Sacramento. Finally, I made it to Donner Summit. My first major hurdle cleared. The vista was spectacular and my spirits rose. It was a perfect, clear day. Mt. Rose, on the horizon to the east, is the highest point in this part of the Sierra and seemed small in the distance. Donner Lake was a blue sapphire glistening down below. The snow sheds covering the railroad snaked along the mountain to the south.

Because the country was engaged in the Civil War, laborers to construct the transcontinental railroad were difficult to find. in the East, the Union Pacific initially solved its labor problem in the east using Irish emigrants, refugees from the Potato Famine, and added ex-soldiers to their crews after the war. But most companies refused to hire the Irish on the East Coast, even with many workers gone fighting the Civil War. It was thought that their

The landmark 1924 Lincoln Highway Rainbow Bridge overlooking Donner Lake.

rowdy leisure activities created problems.

In the West, the Central Pacific hired Chinese to build the railroad. They were excellent workers, didn't strike for better conditions, and would work for lower wages than whites. They were more reliable, peaceful and quiet. They even avoided many of the waterborne illnesses that afflicted the other workers, boiling water for the tea they preferred. In the Sierra they constructed thirteen tunnels, driving through solid granite and shale. The longest was 1,695 feet. The Chinese were called the "Celestials," the heavenly ones, while the Irish became know as the "Terrestrials," the earthy ones.

I started down the hill, crossing the 1924 Rainbow Bridge, a famous Lincoln Highway landmark, before stopping again at the observation area to take some photographs. A monument reminded me that the first pioneer wagons over the Sierra Nevada Mountains arrived here on November 24, 1844. The Stephens-Townsend-Murphy wagon party of fifty men, women and children jumped off from Council Bluffs, Iowa, bound for California on May 22, 1844. A Paiute Indian chief showed them how to reach a river flowing east from the Sierra Nevada which they named Truckee in his honor. Six months of hard travel and they barely made it across the summit before winter closed the pass. Suddenly my two months on a bike didn't seem so difficult.

The ride down to the lake was exhilarating, but I was cautious. I braked frequently to keep my speed down to where I felt reasonably safe. The last thing I needed at this point, after months of planning and preparations, was a crash. I arrived at the bottom refreshed, optimistic and excited. The road along Donner Lake was

beautiful and I rode leisurely, savoring the panorama, the warm weather and the fact that I had made it across the Sierra. At the end of the lake, I stopped at the Donner Monument. I called Nancy and told her I had conquered the summit and would arrive in Truckee in half an hour.

I found the spot where the Breen cabin had stood. They were members of the party of emigrants who started for California from Springfield, Illinois in April of 1846 under the leadership of Captain George Donner. Delays occurred and the party reached this area on October 29, 1846. The Truckee Pass emigrant road had been concealed by snow. The snow depth near this cabin by the lake was twenty-two feet that winter. Ninety people were in the party and forty two perished, most of them from starvation and exposure.

In town, I rode right past Nancy without seeing her and that's difficult to do in a place as small as Truckee. I had only traveled about a block when my phone rang. "Where are you going?" she asked. "I'm just trying to find you," I said. "Look behind you." She was standing out in the street waving at me. As we rode back to Davis, I discovered just how weary and sore I truly was, but I had made it across California.

Climb the mountains and get their good tidings. Nature's peace will flow into you as sunshine flows into trees. The winds will blow their own freshness into you, and the storms their energy, while care will drop off like autumn leaves.

—John Muir

CHAPTER TWO

Nevada

June 4 - Day 6
Truckee to Reno
30.2 miles

I woke at three in the morning, a list of things to do projecting into my brain like a series of slides. I gave up, got up and made notes on a piece of paper. I rummaged around the house checking on maps, lists of names and numbers, camera and film, instruction books, CDs, movies for the VCR – a library of entertainment and information. What had I forgotten? An hour later I gave up and went back to bed only to wake up again at 6:30. A seeming endless array of tasks still remained ranging from a last minute haircut to actually packing the motor home. I had managed a small portion of the packing the day before, but still needed to complete the lion's share. I needed to check in at work, go to the cleaners, and pick up some allergy medicine at the drug store. I was tired and frazzled.

The phone rang continually with well-wishers wanting to say good-bye and chat for a few minutes. A dozen different people dropped by to tour the motor home, offer last minute advice, wish us well, give us a hug and a kiss, and talk for a few minutes. I wasn't sure we would be able to leave at all. It almost proved harder to get out of town than to get over Donner Pass a few days ago, but we would have been disappointed if no one had called or come by to see us off.

Finally we drove out of the driveway and headed east over the ground I had covered the weekend before. It still looked like a lot of uphill travel. The weather was threatening and it appeared to be raining to the north. It had snowed in the mountains a couple days ago. It shouldn't be snowing in June. By the time we arrived in Truckee, we found some sun, but the weather was cool.

I started out of town on a two lane road with no shoulder and a lot of traffic. I thought that situation was difficult until, after a few miles, I turned onto I-80. Here the shoulder was narrow, only five feet wide, and often half-covered in washed out sand and dirt, leaving me less than three feet to ride on. Trucks, buses, cars and motor homes were racing by me just a few feet away. It was Friday and the traffic was heavy. It was, to say the least, an extremely uncomfortable situation for about ten miles. I stopped at one point when I saw a pickup truck parked along an access road next to the river. I

Facing page: Cattle pause to watch a solitary cyclist on old Highway 50 south of Austin.

decided I would either call Nancy or see if I could catch a ride in the back of the pickup. One option was quickly removed when the pickup drove past me onto the freeway – the driver never glancing my way. I finally decided against calling Nancy and continued on, returning to my dangerous pathway, squeezed between the traffic and the guardrail.

At the Nevada border, the road improved dramatically and I thanked God for my deliverance. I vowed to never subject myself to similar conditions again. It simply wasn't worth it. I had anticipated a relatively easy downhill run into Reno, but things hadn't worked out that way. The next ten miles weren't bad, but it was with significant relief that I turned off the intensity of the freeway onto old Highway 40. A few minutes later, I rode into my cousin Tom Stille's garden center and landscape architecture office. I grew up across the street from Tom in a small Iowa town.

Above: Breakfast at the Stilles'. Right: Virginia Street in Reno, center of the "Biggest Little City in the World."

Tom and his wife Kathie took us out for dinner and I easily plowed through a long rack of ribs. The day soon began to catch up with us. Both Nancy and I were exhausted. We returned to our new home on wheels to try out our beds. Nancy had chosen the double bed in the back. I picked the longer mattress located in the front over the cab. It allowed me stretch out my 6'-4" frame without banging my feet against a wall. The disadvantage of my bed was that it was accessed by a ladder. Getting out of bed to use the bathroom during the night without bumping my head on the ceiling or falling off the ladder was going to take some practice.

June 5 - Day 7
Reno to Fallon
64.7 miles

Breakfast in the garden with the Stilles overlooking the swollen Truckee River couldn't have been better. The company, the warm sunshine, the roar of the stream, and a west wind that promised assistance for the journey east all combined to make what should have been a perfect morning. However, storm clouds of doubt and concern were drifting into my sunny thoughts. My right hip hurt – bad. I thought I could ride; I just wasn't sure how far and how much fun it would be. Nancy attempted to treat it by using reflexology. In other words, she exerted pressure on the sciatic nerve in my hip using her thumb or elbow. It might have helped a bit but it was difficult to tell. It certainly hurt, especially when she dug into me with her elbow.

I pedaled into Reno and discovered that my hip was indeed a problem, but it soon dropped into second place on my list of concerns. My rear derailer was not working well. I was having difficulty changing gears and the derailer would regularly slip back and forth from one gear to another, making riding nearly impossible. The casinos on Virginia Street, Reno's main drag, were all open, the noise of the slot machines drifting out into the street. The arch that spans the road reads, "R E N O, The Biggest Little City in the World." It is most impressive at night with all the neon covered casino facades sparkling and flashing behind the sign.

I remembered watching my bike mechanic at home adjust my derailer by turning a nut on the handle bar. I attempted the same procedure, tightening and loosening the cable, but it only seemed to make matters worse. I started thinking about a shorter day, but, on the second day of the trip, it seemed a little early to be changing plans. My mechanical abilities are limited. I can change a tire and have accomplished that task many times. Before I left town, my mechanic showed me how to repair my chain and to replace a spoke. I carried a small tool kit that would permit me to attempt these jobs, but was not confident I could complete either chore.

By the time I reached Sparks, I decided I needed help with my derailer. The next bike shop, after I left town, might be on the other side of Nevada or even in Salt Lake. I turned into a shopping center hoping to find a phone book or someone to direct me to a bike shop. I was looking for a likely place to seek assistance when my luck changed and so did my day. There right in front of me was a bike shop. Inside, a friendly mechanic agreed to help me out immediately and was quickly able to overcome my problem.

Fifteen minutes later, I thanked everyone in the shop and headed east once again. The pain in my leg and hip began to recede, the derailer functioning flawlessly. Soon I was on I-80 following the Truckee River out of town along the railroad tracks. The river created a linear oasis along its banks – trees and green grass stopping

Above: 4th Street in Reno – the old Lincoln Highway and Highway 40.
Below: A Union Pacific freight train heads up the Truckee River east of Reno.

The Ghost River Antique Shop and Museum in Hazen, Nevada

junk attached to the exterior walls, including a couple old bikes. A sign said "open," but the door was locked. Another sign directed me to ring a bell for admittance and a third sign indicated that this was a combination museum and store, with everything for sale. The fine print warned that if you failed to make a purchase, you were required to contribute a buck to the owner.

The proprietor of Ghost River Antiques answered the door. He eventually told that me he used to drive a large truck into San Francisco on a regular basis. He said he would carry a mountain bike with him and, for exercise, would race cable cars up the hills when he had an overnight in the city. He always lost, but one day when he was feeling particularly fit, he actually won. He claimed that the crowd on the cable car was cheering him on the entire way. I have to say that I had my doubts. "Have you been attacked by any cars or trucks?" "No," I answered, "but I did get slapped on the butt about a week ago by a young lady hanging out of the rear window of an old Lincoln." That seemed to impress him. I paid my dollar and cruised down the road toward Fallon.

I stopped in Ragtown, a prominent oasis on the California Emigrant Trail. Located on the banks of the nearby Carson River, Ragtown received its name over a hundred years ago from the pioneer's laundry that would be spread on every handy bush along the river. The forty-mile desert immediately to the north was one of the most dreaded portions of this western trail; Ragtown was the first water stop after the desert. To the thirst-crazed emigrants and their animals, few sights were as welcome as the trees lining the Carson River.

Just north of Fallon, Nancy had parked the motor home in a camp right next to the road, and was waving to me as I rode up. We hooked up the electricity, the water, the sewer and the cable TV. We turned on the hot

abruptly fifty feet on either side of the water at the beginning of the desert. I had entered the Great Basin, the only region in our country where falling water has no outlet to the sea.

I was on a nice downhill run and had a fair breeze at my back. The sun was shining and I was flying. I beat Nancy to Fernly and we had lunch in the motor home. I had forty three miles in the bank and needed only twenty three more to complete my planned route for the day. "No sweat," I thought.

I left the Truckee River behind and followed the road south, stopping to rummage through a junk/antique shop in Hazen. The place had an astonishing appearance from the road with junk machinery and an old pickup parked amid a garden of rusting relics. The building even had

water heater, put a CD into the stereo and popped open a beer. All the luxuries. I showered and changed clothes. Nancy cooked and we enjoyed our first real meal in the motor home. I wasn't prepared to start thinking of New York City, but I was beginning to have visions of Ely, Nevada and that was still over 250 miles away.

June 6 - Day 8
Fallon to Middlegate
53.4 miles

It was cool and overcast, about sixty-five degrees, when I entered Fallon. I stopped to take a few pictures of the town and the old Churchill County courthouse built in 1903. A dilapidated movie theater and a former drug store that now sold western wear were two of the more interesting store fronts on Main Street. The road out of town was flat and progress was smooth. It seemed very much like riding in the Sacramento Valley until, ten miles later, I looked up to see the Stillwater Range looming right in front of me. "Wow," I thought, "where did that come from?" I began to worry that I might have to go straight over it, but the road veered off to the right. I relaxed and stopped worrying about the mountains, when I suddenly heard, and then saw, two large dogs running towards me, inside a fence next to the road. I assumed they would be unable to get out of the yard, but I was soon proven wrong. They dashed through a hole in the fence and ran right at me, growling and barking furiously. They appeared to be totally out of control and intent on having me for breakfast. I panicked, wavering between saying "nice dog" in a sweet voice and screaming "down" in a loud voice. Fortunately, they stopped about three feet away and allowed me to continue on my way. After the pounding of my heart

slowed somewhat, I decided that I needed to develop a plan for dogs and maybe even rehearse it a time or two.

The skies cleared about this time and the temperature jumped ten degrees. It was still quite pleasant. Alfalfa was being harvested in a lush verdant field next to the road. Cottonwood trees were common, their "cotton" drifting in the breeze. Suddenly, a mile later, without warning, I was out in the desert. The green irrigated land, the trees, indeed all civilization simply ended as though God had drawn a line on the ground. Sagebrush and sand now lined the road, tumbleweeds were stacked high against the fences, and the traffic began to thin. I felt like I was finally on Highway 50, the road described by *Life* Magazine as "The Loneliest Road in America." In the article a AAA rep says, "We warn all motorists not to drive there, unless they're confident of their survival skills."

The shoulder was about three feet wide and would have been a perfect place to ride except that grooves had been cut into the surface to create a rumble strip, a warning for vehicles that might be straying off the road. I tried riding on it and thought it wasn't too bad. I could probably manage this across Nevada, but I soon discovered that it wouldn't be necessary. Cars were so infrequent that I just used the traffic lane and would veer onto the shoulder only when an occasional vehicle approached from the rear.

I stopped at Grimes Point, a small anthropological park, to take a path through the desert and view a number of large rocks covered with petroglyphs, meticulous and mysterious artwork of prehistoric people. I walked along past etchings, some created over 7,000 years ago, the scream of Navy jets providing a contrast overhead. This place was not "lonely" when these were carved. It was the shoreline of a huge fresh water sea, Lake Lahontan, and the home to a relatively large popula-

This stretch of highway across Nevada was dubbed the "Loneliest Road in America" by Life *magazine in 1987.*

tion of hunters and gatherers living in homes made of cattails and animal skins. The park proved to be the type of diversion that was perfect for someone on a bicycle, but might not be impressive enough to compel you to stop your car.

I had also hoped to find some water. There was no water at the park, but a man pulled in who was supervising a group of kids on probation. They were picking up garbage along the road. He was happy to give me some of his water. I was glad I asked him for help as I soon discovered that I was going to be on my own for the rest of morning. Towns, gas stations, or even ranches, where I could resupply were going to be few and far between on the trip across Nevada.

Salt Flats was one of the two towns on our map between Fallon and Middlegate. I had thought I might stop and buy a cold drink and take a break. But the only building in Salt Flats turned out to be a legal brothel, a ramshackle one-story building surrounded by a high chain link fence topped by barbed wire and a vast stretch of white alkali desert. There were two large red plastic bows next to a door that had a large heart painted on it.

Nancy smiles while posing in an abandoned car in front of an old stage coach and pony express station in Middlegate.

A women sat on the front steps smoking a cigarette, talking to a guy in a cowboy hat. A sign above them read, "Girls, Girls, Girls." I decided against seeing what kind of soft drinks they might have, although I expected that a visit might have proved interesting. It was a solitary place for a brothel; the only source of possible customers was the Naval Air Base back in Fallon.

A few miles later a sand mountain appeared. It looked like a small piece of the Sahara had been picked up and deposited in Nevada, nestled up against a range of mountains, about a mile off the road. I took a few pictures of the beautiful wind-sculpted shape of the large dune. When I arrived at the road that led back to the dune, I stopped and waited, hoping that Nancy might show up for lunch. However, she arrived just after I left and drove out to take videos of several dune buggies blasting through the sand.

A long uphill awaited me as I left the sand mountain. I could not avoid the mountain range I had hoped to detour around. After climbing for a few miles, I reached the summit. Spread out before me was a wide valley with another range of hills looming in the distance. About halfway across the valley my cell phone rang; it was my daughter, Whitney, calling from New York City. About the time my battery died, Nancy showed up. We had lunch in the motor home with the roar of Navy jets engaged in mock dogfights overhead.

Middlegate, our destination for the day, consisted of a bar and restaurant in a building that was previously an overland stage stop and pony express station. There was also a scattering of mobile homes out back and a small grove of trees on the south side of the building. They even had a hookup for our motor home. We parked amid an amazing collection of junk, ranging from discarded cars and trucks to a group of lifeless appliances, randomly stacked together, resembling a piece of modern art. A hundred yards north of our site was a remnant of the abandoned Lincoln Highway. I cleaned up, took a nap and was later persuaded by Nancy to walk over for a beer. The manager, his wife and another couple were playing pinochle. Three or four guys sat at the bar that was being tended by a friendly woman; a television hung on the wall silently going through the motions. After we ordered our beers, I struck up a conversation with a gaunt-looking fellow. He had long, shoulder-length hair and an impressive mustache. Actually, I just asked a few questions and listened a lot.

Larry spent four years in the Navy stationed on a cruiser that was the flagship for an American admiral in the Mediterranean. "France and England were all right, but you can take the rest of Europe and throw it in the crapper." He claimed his home port, where he had an apartment, was located somewhere near Naples. However, he had never heard of the Amalfi region, located just south of Naples, famous the world over for the narrow, winding drive along the cliffs of the peninsula. He didn't like Italian food (amazing) or the Italian people (even more amazing). He claimed that his job was to drive a thirty-eight foot yacht that the admiral used in port and do little more than lounge around when they were at sea. Larry left the service after four years, spending the last twenty years working for a variety of companies. He was currently unemployed.

He was fixing a generator and overhauling a motorcycle here at Middlegate. But this was only temporary. "As soon as I finish, I'm headed back to Carson City where I live. I need to update my resume and get another job."

"I'm basically an unhappy person." He paused to think about what he'd said, staring at the ceiling, searching for something else to say that would be equally profound. "I've had about a hundred old ladies and even owned a couple houses. But, you know, I was always on the road and, when I'd return, I'd find the windows broken and bums living in them. I just got tired of fixing 'em back up."

Anyway, there was a lot more. I guess I believed some of it, but it was hard to believe all of it.

June 7 - Day 9
Middlegate to Austin
65.2 miles

The old Lincoln Highway weaves through the mountians on its journey to the 7,452' summit east of Middlegate.

Before I left in the morning, I stopped to look at a map I had seen on the wall of the cafe. As I studied it, the owner asked, "Are you going to take the old road?" I said I was concerned with the height of the pass shown on the map, 7,452 feet – higher than Donner Summit in the Sierra. He said, "I think it's the best way to go. All the bikers go that way. I'm pretty sure it's a bit shorter than following Highway 50." So, I decided on the old road and returned to the motor home to give Nancy the new plan. I turned off Highway 50 after four miles onto the road to Eastgate. A little over a mile later, I was sure I had screwed up, but figured it was too late to turn back to the "good road." The asphalt surface was bad and I was climbing already. The Desatoya Mountain Range in front of me looked like the big brother to the one I crossed the day before and I was headed straight into it. It definitely didn't look

good.

After nearly running out of water east of Fallon, I traded my water bottle in for a 70 ounce hydration backpack, called a CamelBak. In addition, my normal luggage consisted of a Canon 35-millimeter camera with a 28-300 mm zoom lens, a small tape recorder, my cell phone and a compact tool kit for my bike. I also carried extra film, sunscreen, a couple spare tubes in case of a flat, a few energy bars, my maps, a credit card, an I.D. and about twenty dollars in cash. It was a light load compared to a cross-cyclist traveling without support and made climbing a little easier for me. Gravity quickly multiplies every extra pound you carried up the mountains of Nevada.

Five miles later, I reached Eastgate, an old mining camp with a large, deserted, limestone house set under tall cottonwoods. There were also several small limestone cottages and outbuildings in various states of ruin where the miners must have lived. To my right the road turned up a beautiful canyon. "Well," I thought. "Today might not be so bad after all." The first four or five miles were wonderful. I was still climbing, but gradually, with a soft breeze at my back. Birds were singing, the stream was gurgling down in the ravine, and there was not a car in sight. (I saw two cars and one motorcycle on my twenty mile trip to the summit.) It was quiet. I now con-

At left: A spectacular view of the Smith Creek Valley and old highway with the snow-covered Shoshone Mountains in the distance. Above: Picture-perfect Carroll Station cattle ranch with a glimpse of a girl riding her horse in a pond.

sidered that my doubts about this road were only a harbinger of adventure. Get out of your rut was the lesson for the day.

When I came out of the canyon, the country expanded – the pungent aroma of sagebrush filling the air. The road in this area, however, was not without its hazards. This was open range. There was a rabbit and a couple of chipmunks that scooted across the road right in front of me. And then, a very large beast appeared, standing right in the middle of the road about a half mile away. It never moved as I approached; it just stood there looking right at me, growing larger. About the time I decided I might need a plan to deal with a very large cow and several calves, the entire herd turned and ran off the road, down into a draw.

The next five or six miles were difficult, but the country was beautiful. I began climbing through a pine for-est. Nancy passed me and agreed to wait with lunch about ten miles up the road. I thought I'd be there in less that an hour, but I underestimated the degree of difficulty I was facing. The grade was very steep, and the altitude was not helping. It felt like that cow had climbed onto the back of my bike. The only good news was that the temperature was still in the sixties and there was a tangy smell of the piñon pine forest in the air. A tenth of a mile became a victory – a mile a triumph. Every twist of the road promised me a view of the crest, but I was disappointed time and time again. Struggling along at not much over four miles an hour – barely fast enough to keep the bike in an upright position – I finally reached the summit.

The downhill side was great and, five wild miles later, I spotted the motor home down below. It was parked just off the road, looking out on a range of snow-covered mountains that spread in front of me as far as I could see. A long, straight, empty two-lane ribbon of blacktop ran down the hill and vanished into the distance on the other side of the wide, green valley. Just below us was Carroll Station, a cattle ranch that would look good on the cover of Ranch Magazine. We watched a teenaged girl ride her horse back and forth in the shal-

Above: Snow melt feeds Schoonover Creek east of Middlegate. At right: A cemetary on Highway 50 below Austin.

lows of small pond. Her younger brother was tearing around on a tiny four-wheel vehicle. Our lunch was delicious and we both decided it was going to be difficult to find a place to eat with a more beautiful vista.

Forty miles still remained and I was more than a little tired, but at least I was going downhill for the next several miles. I crossed the valley and then turned north and continued up the east side. There was another small range of hills to cross. The valley to the north was also spectacular – more ranch land, still green with spring. Water was running everywhere and ducks flapped away as I approached. No cars were in sight and the snowy mountains dominated the landscape to the east. The wind was at my back again and I was making good time.

I returned to Highway 50, just a couple miles west of Austin, and found a problem. There was another steep uphill push and it was coming at a bad time, late in a

long hard day. I stopped and removed my shoes from my aching feet. My feet would swell in my shoes, straining against the laces. This swelling while pushing on the pedals created a tourniquet around my feet causing me discomfort. After of few minutes, my feet felt better. I was able to return my shoes to my feet and struggle up the grade a mile or so, stopping at a cemetery to take some pictures and rest a bit. I admired an angel that surmounted a stone dating from the late 1800s. The angel pointed her sword up the road towards the town, reminding me that I had a way to go before my day would be complete. I returned to my bike and pushed up the final hill, right through the main street of town, where I found Nancy waiting for me. She was parked a short distance from two venerable bars, The Owl Club and The Last Chance Saloon. I was too tired to take time to check them out.

We sat in the motor home, sharing a cold drink. She told me what she had learned about Austin while waiting for me to arrive. Austin is laid out at the bottom of a canyon and it had snowed here less than a week ago. Houses south of the road, in the shadow of the mountains, rarely experience sunshine from November until May. Most of the structures, including three of the four high-steepled churches that dominate the architecture of Austin, are built north of the road and enjoy a better exposure. A storekeeper told her that he had slipped on a piece of ice in the shady part of town in December, spraining his wrist in the process. Four months later he had slipped on the same piece of ice, injuring his hip. He was nearly recovered and told her, "I'm not going back up there again until August, and only then if someone goes up there first to make sure that ice is gone!"

I followed Nancy another mile up the hill to our camp. I should have enjoyed my victory over those mountains, but I began to wonder what the next day might have in store for us.

June 8 - Day 10
Austin to Eureka
70.8 miles

A high altitude day. The map showed that I would start the day at 6,577 feet, ride over two high passes in Toiyabe Range – 7,484 and 7,254 feet respectively – and then finish over seventy miles away in Eureka to spend the night at 6,200 feet. The temperature was cool, in the low fifties when I started. The road left Austin the same way it came in, climbing steeply up the mountain. I passed the Loneliest Bike Store in America just above camp. About a mile up the road I saw another bike rider just preparing to get back on the road. Mike Thieroff had started his trip in San Francisco and was on his way back home to Toledo, Ohio. He planned to pass through Utah, Colorado and Kansas. We agreed to struggle up the hill together and ride on to Eureka. It was good to have someone to talk and share stories with. He looked fit, lean and sun-burned, with a handsome, prominent nose and irresistible, enthusiastic personality. Mike was exactly my age, a 57 year old retired high school principal. He was on his third cross country trip. The first long ride carried him from San Diego to Tampa, the second from Oregon to Ohio. He had also made a number of shorter treks.

Mike obviously loved it. "What a beautiful day!" "Look at this land!" "What a great country!" These were

Travelling companion and bike nut Mike Theiroff.

Eureka, Nevada with the venerable old Opera House built in 1880.

typical of his frequent exclamations. Mike was fully independent, carrying everything he needed with him and spending the nights in motels. He ate breakfast and dinner in restaurants, and carried his lunch and snacks with him. His larder consisted of juice, pretzels, nuts, raisins, fruit and an occasional can of beans, corn or spinach. He packed efficiently. He only had about thirty pounds of gear plus seven full water bottles.

Back in 1884, Thomas Stevens also left on a cross-country trip from San Francisco – just as Mike and I did. The twenty-nine year old transplanted Englishman took the ferry *Alameda* across the bay to Oakland on April 22, where a crowd of friends and well-wishers waved good-bye to him as he rode north following San Pablo Avenue on his "ordinary," the most popular bicycle of the day. It had a fifty-inch front wheel, with the pedals attached directly to it, and a sixteen-inch back wheel. It took him a little over four months to travel 3,700 miles and finally reach Boston, becoming the first person to bicycle across the United States. Given the condition of the roads at that time, I'm amazed he reached Reno, let alone the East Coast. He carried his food and clothing in a pack on his back. He managed to escape a snow storm in the high Sierra, a mountain lion in Nevada and flooded streams throughout the west. After Boston, he sailed to England, rode across Europe and Asia and arrived back in San Francisco on January 4, 1887, having covered over 13,500 miles on his bike. He was a national hero and one of our first bike nuts. Mike and I didn't run into any mountain lions.

I invited Mike for lunch in the motor home. Nancy arrived a little after eleven and I introduced her to Mike. She continued up the road to a turnout and we arrived about twenty minutes later. The delicious lunch, featuring turkey sandwiches, made me appreciate the luxury of my existence compared to the hardy bikers, like Mike, who labor across the country on their own. The physical support of having someone carry all my gear, books, maps, food and clothes, not to mention the peace of mind of having someone just a phone call away if I had mechanical or weather problems was important. It certainly made my trip easier – perhaps even made it possible.

After lunch, another grade, another grind, another pass above 7,000 feet. The afternoon was long because we had only managed twenty-five miles before lunch time. My son Eric was able to get through on my cell phone as we were crossing a wide valley. He had a business question and we discussed it while I gazed out across the wide open spaces of the Great Basin. Nancy also called twice, once to tell Mike she had secured him a motel room and, a second time, to find out what had happened to us. We were running behind schedule.

My right hip ached again and my butt was really sore. Mike complained of a few aliments as well. Misery loves company. He should be tired – he had ridden all the way to Austin from Fallon the day before, a distance of over 110 miles. It was after four when we rode up a steep grade into Eureka. Why did every day have to end with a climb? I was also very tired – fried, burnt to a crisp, despite several applications of sun block.

Nancy was waiting on the main street and had scouted out the town. She had even managed to secure "Pony Express Country" T-shirts for all three of us from the manager of the old Eureka Opera House. Mike and I hurried over to thank him and take a quick tour of the building. Across the street, facing the opera house that was built in 1880, was the old courthouse with a Lincoln Highway marker in front. Eureka had preserved several interesting pieces of its mining town history.

A good camp with a hot shower and a chicken dinner was another mile and half up the road. I made it, just barely. After dinner, I slumped in a chair – my evening entertainment watching four or five deer grazing a couple hundred yards above the camp. After the sun went down, the view of the surrounding mountains dimmed, lit only by the light of the bright stars.

June 9 - Day 11
Eureka to Ely
79.4 miles

Mike arrived at our door a little after 6:30 and found that I wasn't quite ready. We invited him in out of the cold while I ate my omelette and finished getting ready. We started our day climbing again through the Fish Creek Range, uphill towards the summit of the first of four passes, three over 7,000 feet high. After crawling slowly to the top, we discovered that the wind that had been chasing us across the state of Nevada was now blowing out of the east. It was going to be necessary to work our way down the hills as well as up.

We pedaled through a roller-coaster series of mountains and valleys, pushing into the wind. The mountain ranges here in Nevada seemed to be still rising, pushing out of the desert as we struggled up their flanks, newer than the established Sierra Nevada. Nancy caught up with us after our second summit and we stopped to eat on the way up to the third. We had only completed 32 miles by lunch. With the wind and the long climbs, we were tired. Nancy read a book while Mike and I took short naps, needing to recharge our batteries.

The fourth climb was brutal, about ten miles long and over two thousand feet of climbing. Halfway up, I was surprised to hear my phone ring. It was my understanding that cell phones weren't supposed to work here in the wilderness between Reno and Salt Lake. But it was Nancy offering to meet us about fifteen miles from Ely for a change to rest and refuel. She was parked at the top of the last pass of the day. In California history, the "Big 4," were Crocker, Huntington, Hopkins and Stanford, the California railroad barons. But after this most difficult day, this Californian will remember the *really* big 4 – Pinto Summit at 7,376 feet, Pancake Summit at 6,521 feet, Little Antelope Summit at 7,438 feet, and Robinson Summit at 7,607 feet.

The day had turned cloudy and cool as we prepared to resume our ride and we worried about rain. Clouds began to cover the sky, streaming in from the west. We each threw on an extra jersey and started down the hill into the breeze. The ride to Ely took a little over an hour and featured sore butts and tired bodies. My feet and hands weren't very happy either. It was my most difficult day – nearly 80 miles and four high passes, over seven hours on the bike, much of it into the wind.

Mike treated us to dinner in Ely before we headed out to our camp. We will start north tomorrow toward Wendover while he stays on Highway 50 headed southeast. As we shook hands and said our good-byes, he captured what we were both feeling when he said, "You know, I feel like I've known you both all my life." We had exchanged many of our best stories during the two days we had struggled across Nevada's mountainous Great Basin together.

Ely suffered when compared with Eureka. Ely was bigger, still an active mining town, with 600 hotel or motel rooms and several moderate sized casinos, anchored by the Nevada Club on a corner of the main drag. There was a shortage of charm, but Nancy did enjoy visiting the railroad museum in the afternoon. We had cable TV back in the camp and, after a long hot shower, I enjoyed chocolate ice cream while watching the Knicks beat the Pacers.

June 10 - Day 12
Ely to Lages Station
57.5 miles

A different day, a different beginning. The road was smooth, sloping gently upward, with a wide shoulder. Traffic was light to moderate. The only problem was a persistent head wind. I had worried about a north wind on this stretch of road when I was at home planning the trip. My concern proved prophetic.

The first ten miles passed smoothly and, it wasn't long before I jumped off my bike to stretch my legs in the town of McGill. It was a nice looking little town with houses that were all cut from the same pattern – cottages with hip roofs. All were brightly painted, well maintained and had gardens planted with flowers. They must have all been built by a mining company for their workers and their families. Downtown, with a main street that had seen better times, featured an old movie theater, closed; a grocery store, boarded up; and a couple of lodge halls, used occasionally. There was also Marie's

Restaurant, a beauty shop, the post office and a few other businesses scattered along both sides of the highway. Just past the business district was an old empty, brick school and brand new LDS church. The church building was gorgeous and surrounded by over an acre of lush, manicured lawn. I had arrived in Mormon country. That might also explain why the houses had looked so good.

I was going "with the grain" across Nevada as I rode north. Prominent mountain ranges marched along either side of me as I proceeded up the middle of the wide valley. It was very different from the last several days, when I had traveled "against the grain," crossing range after range of mountains. This was better, except, of course, for the wind.

Thirty miles from Ely, I glanced out to my right and saw what I thought was a hat on top of a post. One advantage of riding a bike is that it's so easy to stop and

Left: Club 50 Cafe north of Ely.
Right: A mysterious, one-of-a-kind roadside memorial to Michael Tillery.

take a look at something along the road; to read an historical marker, to take a picture of an old restaurant or gas station, or to investigate a hat on a post. The hat on the post turned out to be a memorial to a Michael Tillery who was born in 1954 and died in 1994. It was a simple iron cross, about two feet high, painted white with his name and the dates imprinted into the iron. There was an amazing collection of caps – maybe twenty or twenty-five – hanging on it. I was intrigued by a Monday Night Football cap with ABC TV embroidered on the back. Had Michael been an ABC employee? It was a moving memorial, but the mystery remained. Who was Michael Tillery, what happened to him at forty years of age out here on this lonely road, and where did all the hats come from?

The wind turned out to be a herald for increasing clouds, which were followed by scattered showers and stronger winds. I could see rain squalls all around me – several storms moving across the sky like huge ships. I judged, optimistically, that things looked better ahead. Not necessarily, I discovered. The road was wet and sporadically the wind would blow hard. I managed to miss most of the showers, but none of the wind. The temperature dropped from 75° to 65° when the showers blew through. It was brisk, especially with the stronger winds. Fortunately I was working hard enough to keep warm.

I avoided one rather prolonged bit of rain when Nancy caught up with me for lunch. We sat eating while the rain pinged against the hard roof of the motor home. Good timing. I wasn't able to avoid an increasingly sore rear end, despite the fact that I worked hard every evening and every morning doing all I could to take proper care of it. The effort included baths, dry clothing, and various ointments and salves. What I really needed was callouses.

The day was short and ended just shy of sixty miles. When I planned the trip, I had anticipated more time to explore the countryside and towns we visited. The challenge of getting from one town to the next while crossing Nevada had pretty much drained my tank, as well as used up most of the day. Now, with my conditioning improved and the demands of distance and elevation decreased, I had a little more time. I arrived in Lages Station before three o'clock. If Lages Station had been more than a general store with camping facilities at the junction of two highways, we could have tested my theory.

June 11 - Day 13
Lages Station to Wendover
59.8 miles

Gloria is nine years old and lives with her father and mother in an old trailer in Lages Station. Ely is sixty miles to the south and Wendover is sixty miles to the north; so she lives in the middle of nowhere. She decided this morning that she would ride on her bike with me to Wendover. I first saw her small pink and white bike when I rode into the park the day before. She had come out of her home and had asked me, "What are you doing? Where are you going on that bike?" I told her and, because I saw that she had a bike, I invited her to ride with me the next day.

In the morning, as soon as she saw me take my bike off the rack, she raced outside and jumped on her bike. She was wearing cowboy boots with lots of fringe on the back. "Now you have to wait for me. I don't ride very fast and I won't be able to go all the way." Luckily she was distracted by a little friend as I was making preparations to leave and they went over near his trailer to play. I managed to sneak away.

I rode for three miles with no vehicles passing me in either direction. My phone rang and I spent fifteen minutes talking to my brother Chuck back home in

Davis. The news was nearly all good, but right near the end of the conversation, I sustained an injury. I was sort of sitting or leaning on my bike, between the handle bars and the seat. Suddenly my front wheel turned and the bike began to move out from under me. As I attempted to catch myself, the bike chain slashed across the back of my right calf. It wasn't a deep cut and didn't even hurt very much, but it was bleeding pretty good. I decided to blame the injury on my brother rather than my careless use of the bike as a chair. (It turned out to be my most serious injury of the trip and left a two-inch scar on my leg – a lasting reminder of the journey.)

The morning had clear skies, mild temperatures and a wind that continued to impede my progress. Two passes stood between me and Wendover. Neither was a monster, but both demanded that I get over the 6,000 foot level and both made me wish they were lower and shorter. The old road, the Lincoln Highway, seemed to follow along on one side of the highway or the other for almost the entire day. In Nevada, they never throw an old road away, they just build a new one next to it. I had spent the last couple weeks looking for pieces of the old highway as I biked along. Now, I could see that the old road was narrow and had to follow the contours of the land much more closely than today's model. There were only very modest cut-and-fill sections, compared to the road I was on.

I stopped to see if I could help two families gathered next to their pickups stopped by the side of the road, one with the hood up. They had the problem fixed. They thanked me and even offered me a ride. I declined and later wondered what it was that I would have been able to do for them. I am not a great mechanic. Maybe I could have made a call on my cell phone. Riding on a bike returned me to a different era, a time when people weren't afraid and could offer each other assistance.

A view of the old Lincoln Highway, abandoned in the desert.

The first view of the vast ocean of white, the Great Salt Desert east of Wendover.

I came down from the second pass, turned a corner and looked off to the east. Out in the distance was a vast expanse devoid of color – a flat, endless, glistening ocean of white. It was my first view of the Great Salt Lake Desert, the desert I planned to cross the next day. I was impressed, excited and more than a little nervous. I could see why the early pioneer wagon trains were so concerned about crossing this deadly region. The broad shimmering plain seemed to extend almost without end. The Rockies, far off in the distance to the east, seemed small in comparison. It looked formidable.

Jedediah Smith was the first white man to cross the Great Basin in 1827 on his way back from California, following a route similar to mine. He and a companion nearly died crossing this desert that stretched before me. They subsisted on horse meat, were tormented by thirst and even buried themselves in sand to cool their bodies. Finally, on June 27, their struggle ended when they arrived at the Great Salt Lake.

John Fremont had better luck when he left headed west from Salt Lake with Kit Carson as his guide in late October of 1845. Carson wrote, *"We travelled on about*

60 miles, no water or grass, not a particle of vegetation could be found, as level and bare as a barn floor, before we struck the mountains."

Fremont and Carson continued across Nevada on a line close to my Highway 50 route. The winter snows were late that year and they were able to cross the Sierra at Donner Pass. Fremont and his party of fifteen men hitched their horses at Captain Sutter's fort in present day Sacramento on December 9.

Just before Wendover, I was coasting down a nice incline when I noticed an old reddish Dodge Challenger in my rear view mirror. It had yellow and orange flames painted on the hood that were badly faded. When it didn't zoom past me, I looked again. The car seemed to be slowing down, almost like it was stalking me, and soon pulled up close behind me. Now what? I had imagined many times just how I might react if someone attempted to rob or assault me. I could never decide if I should, or would have to, give them everything: my phone, my camera and my bike, as well as the twenty dollars I normally carried with me. I wondered if they'd allow me to keep the film in my camera. I wondered if I shouldn't just drop everything and run off into the nearest field. There was no one around and I felt totally vulnerable.

When the vehicle pulled up beside me, I stopped my bike and peered into the car. All the windows were down and a guy with a skimpy blond mustache was at the wheel. Two girls sat in the front seat, both smoking. Two more girls were in the back, one smoking. All of them were young and wearing tee-shirts. It looked like it wasn't going to be a stickup. "Where you coming from on that bike?" asked the guy. "San Francisco," I answered. "Wow! How long did it take you to get here?" asked one of the girls in the front seat as she attempted to flick her ash out the window. It landed on the girl next to her. Neither appeared to be bothered by the care-

less act; maybe they were used to it. "About ten days," I answered. "Really, how old are you?" asked a girl in the back seat. (In other words, "What's a guy your age doing out riding around on a bicycle.") "Fifty-seven," I said. "Are you married?" "Yeah," I answered, a little surprised by the question. "Where's your wife?" "I hope she's in Wendover finding us a place to spend the night. Where arc you guys from?" "Oh, wc're from Wendover. Well, have a good ride." They left me going sixty down the highway. I plugged along, going fifteen.

As I approached town, I could see evidence again of I-80 and the transcontinental railroad. I'd be back traveling with these two faithful companions, having left them a half a day out of Reno. Nancy found a modern, but barren, RV park next to a large casino. It was hot in the sun, with pavement surrounding the vehicle, and we turned on the air conditioner for the first time. I set up the barbecue and plugged the television into the outlet on the side of the motor home. After the sun ducked behind the high-rise hotel next door, I relaxed in a lawn chair and watched another NBA playoff game.

After the game we walked to the strip and visited the casino next door. The giant neon cowboy, "Wendover Will," stood in front along the road, soaring sixty-four feet into the night sky, giving a friendly wave to all that passed by. Will has been a part of the landscape in Wendover since the early fifties. The nine-ton cowboy was standing on a red and white sign that made the claim, "WHERE THE WEST BEGINS." I couldn't quite agree, since that would put states like Colorado and Wyoming in the Midwest. We didn't stay long inside. There was nothing in Wendover that we hadn't seen many times before in Reno or Lake Tahoe, and the desert had to be crossed tomorrow, the last barrier standing between us and a rest day in Salt Lake City.

Wendover Will points the way.

Bring me men to match my mountains,
Bring me men to match my plains ...

—Sam Walter Foss

CHAPTER THREE

Utah

June 12 - Day 14
Wendover to Tooele, Utah
77.1 miles

I hadn't slept well, primarily because I was clearly concerned about the day that lay in front of me. I wanted to make an early start to beat the heat and make some miles before the winds picked up. At seven in the morning it was 59° and I was making good time. Traffic was light – very different than the traffic on Interstate 80 back in California – maybe one truck a minute. I began to think I might arrive in Salt Lake City, on the other side of this vast expanse of white, shortly after noon.

About seven miles out of town, I found myself taking pictures in the desert of water birds. Something I wouldn't have predicted. The winter snows and spring rains had left the desert covered with water. Before long I could see the Bonneville Salt Flats stretching off to the north. I remembered when I came through

here back in the sixties on one of my trips between California and my home back in Iowa. A buddy and I drove all night, taking turns at the wheel. We stopped for breakfast in Wendover at a diner on the east side of town, right before the desert. Wendover was a very different place then, much smaller, with few, if any, casinos, certainly none of the giant pleasure palaces that exist today. As we ate, we began to notice that several of the people in the diner were wearing jump suits with patches on them, outfits that I immediately associated with auto racing. We discovered that they were part of a crew attempting to break the land speed record. It was exciting to be a small part of the grand enterprise. They looked and acted like celebrities and were on their way to Bonneville to prepare for their day.

Twenty miles out there was still lots of water. I stopped and walked over to check the surface of the

Above: The mountains reflecting in the water covering the Bonneville Salt Flats.
Left: Shorebirds in the desert, a pair of avocets east of Wendover.
Facing page: The Wasatch Mountains tower above Salt Lake.

A highway memorial.

desert with my foot in a relatively dry area. It was soft. It felt like my bike might sink into the white mud several inches. There would be no speed records on Bonneville on this day. This condition was a major problem for the pioneers who arrived early in the year to this region. They would sink up to the axles of their wagons or, many years later, of their automobiles. A wagon train would have to wait until the sand dried up and turned into the hard, flat surface that the racers loved. Eventually a causeway solved the problem for the highway, just as it had some years earlier for the railroad.

Bonneville is also the location where world speed records for bicycles were set. In 1986, John Howard, following closely behind a wind screen connected to a racing vehicle, was able to ride 152 miles per hour. In 1993, Fred Rumpleberg was nearly killed when he crashed after slipping out from behind his moving screen at 140 miles per hour. He returned three years later to set a new world record of 167 miles per hour.

I would have been thrilled with a tenth of that speed. A couple of hours into the trip, the wind that had plagued me for the last three days returned. Sometimes, it seemed to blow more from the north than the east, but never at my back where I needed it. It was frustrating. I had worried about this stretch of road back home, but I had never visualized it with a head wind. Give me a mountain any day. You can conquer a mountain. After a finite ascent you were even rewarded with a downhill run. I couldn't vanquish the wind anymore than I could defeat a broken leg. I could only endure it.

I expected Nancy to catch up with me half way across this wilderness. Signs along the road said, "Emergency Parking Only." Where was I going to rest my tired body if we couldn't park? But at mile post 41, there was an exit and the problem was solved. Ten minutes later Nancy arrived, just I as finished changing the tube in my rear tire. I had suffered my first flat tire as I pulled onto the off-ramp. One flat every 750 miles would be very acceptable.

The mountains of Nevada that had delighted and plagued me over the last many days were now just a hazy outline, barely visible above the western horizon. They didn't seem nearly so significant when viewed from here. But my memories of them were still fresh, not at all hazy. The major feature in the landscape, at this point, was in front of me, the rising wall of mountains to the east, signaling the beginning of the Rockies. At this point, the desert had changed into range land, not all that different from the land I had traveled through in Nevada.

The land forms also resembled Nevada in another way – ranges of mountains, running north to south in front of me, obstructing my progress. The highway turned from its straight eastern course and headed north to avoid the snow-capped portions of the first range. The objective was to climb over the tails or toes of these ranges. Unfortunately, they had long tails and big toes. So after fifty-some miles of head-winds on dead flat ground, I now had to start climbing.

Each range concealed a loftier one that seemed to be hiding behind the preceding one and I still was not in sight of the Wasatch Mountains that form the major barrier to the east of Salt Lake. At freeway exit 77, seventy-seven miles into Utah, I threw in the towel, called Nancy and asked her to pick me up. I was hot and tired and simply didn't want to pedal anymore. She met me, we drove east about twenty miles and checked into a motel for the night. I showered and instantly fell asleep while she went shopping.

That evening we walked a block to the TA Travel Center, a monster truck stop. Over a hundred of the eighteen-wheeled behemoths were parked bumper-to-bumper, side-by-side in formation throughout the parking lot. They resembled a horde of dinosaurs gathered at a water hole. Engines growled, keeping refrigerated cargo cool. Another cluster of semis was lined up six or seven deep in two lines, waiting to fill their tanks with diesel. It was impossible not to be impressed when a big Peterbilt roared by me on the Interstate – forty tons moving at seventy-five miles an hour. Walking along next to this collected concentration of power – gleaming chrome radiators and glistening steel tractors, painted in every bright color of the rainbow – was overwhelming.

The inside of the restaurant was an oven. The owner had remodeled the place in the spring and added a row of west facing windows, but had not yet received the blinds to cover them. The late afternoon sun slammed into the room with the force of a blast furnace. Two women, who were waiting tables in our section, looked like they had just finished riding with me from Wendover. They looked exhausted, hot and tired, with eyes that stared at their customers almost without recognition. We found a booth in the corner that seemed to be the only place in the room not in the direct path of the sun.

The diners were primarily men, presumably truckers, and they were large. Some were just big, others fat, some both. Nancy couldn't get over it. "Look at that one! The guy by the salad bar is huge." He was; they all were. There was an announcement on the intercom. I told Nancy I thought they were paging a trucker, "I bet they take really good care of those guys here."

A guy in the booth next to us who had overheard me said, "Aw, they just want someone to move their rig up in the gas line. They don't care a lick about drivers here and neither do the owners of the trucks for that matter. They only want that load transferred and could care less about the drivers." In addition to the unhappy trucker and the unhappy waitresses, I found an unhappy cashier when I tried to buy a newspaper and a candy

A horde of eighteen-wheelers parked outside the TA Travel Center near Salt Lake City.

bar while paying for our meal. I was standing in the wrong place, the phone had rung and there wasn't a price on the newspaper. Nancy and I walked out laughing, happy to escape.

June 13 - Day 15
Tooele to Salt Lake
49.3 miles

Nancy dropped me back at mile post 77. It was a discouraging drive back from mile post 99 where we had spent the night. Retreating didn't feel good. That first 22 miles would take me from the tip of one mountain range to the tip of another, across the end of Tooele Valley. The Interstate and the railroad had taken a shortcut across a bay of the Great Salt Lake. The bay was an extension of this valley that lay just to

An old post card view of a group of bathers at the Saltair Pavilion, circa 1900.

the south. There was a causeway, about a fifteen miles long, that connected one side with the other.

This shortcut turned out to be a major headache several years ago. Salt Lake was rising due to heavy snowfall in the mountains. High storm waters shut down both the railroad and I-80, two vital arteries. The federal government built a huge, expensive pumping station that attempts to keep the level of the lake down by pumping water into the desert.

Birds were numerous for the first few miles and a couple of large, noisy, black ones were actually chasing me away. They flew along above me, dive bombing my red helmet. It stimulated me to push harder against the wind that was still in my face. All along this piece of road you could see where people had spelled out messages with rocks in the sand. "Dick ♥ Mary" or "I love Denise." All the messages were submerged in a foot or two of water. I guessed that it must dry up here significantly in the summer. If the weather continued as hot as it has been here the last couple days, it wasn't going to take very long.

The last few miles of causeway ran along next to a beautiful marsh. I must have flushed over a dozen pairs of mallards as I rode along. They didn't pay any attention to the cars and trucks, but were not taking any chances with me. It reminded me that Karl Malone, star basketball player with the Utah Jazz, was a duck hunter. After the Jazz had slipped by the Sacramento Kings in game four of the playoff series he was interviewed on

television, inviting all his duck hunting buddies to bring their duck calls for the final game in Salt Lake.

I finally caught up with Nancy at exit 104 for a drink and a snack. My ears were again becoming a little crispy. In fact, the top of my right ear was starting to resemble a potato chip. My right side was constantly exposed to the sun, since I was generally heading east and the sun was typically to the south. Nancy found some zinc oxide to help provide protection.

Across the freeway to the north, from where we were parked, was the Great Salt Lake and a huge dance pavilion called Saltair. The original Saltair Pavilion was a turn of the century wonder. It resembled a Moorish palace with an arched facade and domed turrets and was served by its own rail line. Two thousand people came to dance in the main ballroom. It also featured a large theater, bathing in the lake and a Coney Island style amusement park. The old building was still around when I drove through here in the sixties. At that time it was a derelict, crumbling in ruin, sitting out in the lake, isolated by flood waters, far from the shore line. Even in that state, it looked far better than the cheap imitation that was its current replacement.

I cruised off the Interstate and started into the city, the breeze behind me. Thank God. It felt good to be off that busy road. It felt good to be across Nevada and the Great Salt Lake Desert. I had made it to Salt Lake City on schedule – an important landmark for me. The past ten days of continuous difficult biking had been a significant uncertainty as I planned the trip. Would the conditioning I had managed in the spring be adequate? As it turned out, the answer was "Just barely." The other really wonderful news was that we planned to take the next day off and visit the city, a day of rest and recovery before starting up into the Rockies. As I looked at that formidable barrier of Wasatch Mountains looming to the east of Salt Lake – jagged, ominous, their peaks covered with snow – I knew that day off was important.

Meriwether Lewis had similar concerns when he viewed the Rocky Mountains for the first time. *"When I reflected on the difficulties which this snowy barrier would probably throw in my way to the Pacific, and the sufferings and hardships of myself and party in them, it in some measure counterbalanced the joy I had felt in the first moments in which I gazed on them."* I also was happy to have the Rockies in sight, and shared his doubts about the hardships that were ahead in the mountains.

I met Nancy one more time for lunch in a park right on the road. The remainder of the ride was short with a fair amount of traffic on city streets, four lanes or more wide. I was glad to be crossing the city on Sunday; it would have been bad to ride those roads during the week. We found a good camp and filled up with LP gas. We had run out of gas using our heater during the cold nights in the mountains. Our refrigerator, which uses LP gas when we are not hooked up to electricity, was warming up swiftly on this hot day.

June 14 - Day 16
Salt Lake City
Rest Day

The morning started with a pancake breakfast and, since neither of us were moving very fast, I had some time to catch up with my journal. About ten o'clock we decided to leave the motor home in camp, connected to its services, and ride our bikes into town. At this large, modern camp in Salt Lake we had electricity, water, sewer and cable TV. So disconnecting and storing all the cables, hoses and cords takes some doing, and I would then have to unpack and reconnect when

we returned. We also didn't want to expose our home to theft and vandalism if we parked on the street in the city. We were both bike riders for the day.

We first stopped by the Union Pacific Railroad station, a wonderful old building in need of renovation. It was closed. Just down the street was the Rio Grande Depot that was beautifully restored. It housed the Amtrak ticket office and the Utah State Historical Society Museum. The museum proved to be a real find. It had excellent exhibits on pioneer wagon trains, the transcontinental railroad and even the Lincoln Highway. There was the old iron sign that

Top: Union Pacific Station.
Below: Old post card of Salt Lake with the Rocky Mountains in the distance.

had marked the place where the highway crossed from Utah into Nevada, some great photos of guys installing Lincoln Highway signs in downtown Salt Lake back in the twenties, and a variety of other memorabilia. There was also a section with old photos and post cards of the Saltair Pavilion when it was in full swing.

I was impressed when I read a quote from a pioneer women who had made the trip across country. On May 2, 1851, Jean Rio Baker wrote, *"We have traveled some few miles every day, and are now stopped by a snow storm, and the cold is so great, we are glad to take refuge in our wagons; do not expect me to describe our road, as they call it, it is a perfect succession of hills, valleys, bogs, mudholes, log bridges, quagmires, with stumps of trees, a foot above the surface of the watery mud, so that without the utmost care, the wagons would be overturned, ten times a day."*

Just off the main room of the depot was an old restaurant, also wonderfully restored. The stools around its central soda fountain were gorgeous – all of them appeared to be original, with high wooden backs and red plastic seats. There was a large Rio Grande Railroad logo on one wall in pink neon. It was a classy place, but a little early for lunch. We were tempted.

We rode back by the Delta Center, home of the Utah Jazz basketball team. The Rio Grande depot and the Delta Center, have started a renaissance in this part of town. One block of old buildings was occupied by architects, interior designers and attractive shops. The area reminded me of a smaller, western version of New York City's Soho.

Just north of Salt Lake, near Ogden, is Promontory Point, the historic spot where the transcontinental railroad was completed. The construction of the railroad began with one company headed east out of Sacramento and the other west from Omaha. No point had been decided for the meeting of the two routes and each company struggled to cover as much ground as possible. Each mile they completed meant more grant money from the government for their owners and less for the competing railroad. There was a contest during the final months to see which railroad could build the fastest. Central Pacific crews managed to lay over ten miles of track on April 29, 1869, in just twelve hours. The duel ended at Promontory Summit, fifty-six miles west of Ogden. The two company presidents, Leland Stanford of the Central Pacific and Thomas Durant of the Union Pacific, both attempted mighty blows to drive in the ceremonial "golden spike." To the great amusement of the two crews, both missed. The race had captured the imagination of all Americans. On May 10, 1869, the message flew by telegraph to both the Atlantic and the Pacific coasts: "Done!" The

The spires of the Mormon Tabernacle soar high over Temple Square.

world's first transcontinental railroad was complete.

We locked our bikes in front of Salt Lake City's main attraction, Temple Square and the Mormon Tabernacle. We were disappointed to find that we couldn't visit the temple unless we were members of the Church of Latter-Day Saints. Nancy managed to attend an organ recital in Assembly Hall and thought it was great. I liked the monument to the sea gull. The first summer after the Mormon pioneers arrived in this area, their crops were attacked by a swarm of locusts. The pioneers fought valiantly, since their crops were the only thing that would prevent them from starving. They were losing the battle to the insects when a massive flock of sea gulls showed up, devouring all the trespassers and saving the day. Today, the sea gull is Utah's state bird.

We walked past the Hotel Utah and discovered that it wasn't a hotel. Inside, we were greeted by a women standing next to the door. Nancy learned that the hotel was acquired over time by members of the LDS church who purchased shares of stock in the hotel. Eventually, they owned the whole thing. They shut down the hotel operation, refurbished the place and now use it for wedding receptions. The Tabernacle across the street has several weddings every day, and we noticed a schedule indicating three wedding luncheons and four wedding dinners on this particular Monday.

Just a block past the hotel was the Beehive House, the home of Brigham Young. We took the tour and found a great example of a house built in the last half of the 1800s, with furnishings of the period, many of which actually belonged to the Young family. We learned that old Brigham had been quite a guy, founder of the Mormon Church, the first governor of the state and the father of fifty-six children. And I thought I had my hands full with two. The tour was a little long. Before it finished, we got hungry, managed to duck out and dash across the street for a bite to eat.

Our next stop was Guthries, a store that claimed to be one of the 100 biggest bike shops in the United States. I needed some spare tubes for my bike as my front tire had gone flat on me the day before. Now it was two flats in two days, not one flat in 800 miles, a very different proposition. I suspected that my recent rash of flat tires was directly related to the use of the Interstate highway system. The shoulder glittered with small bits of broken glass as I rode along. I was also warned about small wires, debris from the steel-belted tires used on the large semi-trucks and trailers.

We decided to ride up into an older neighborhood with many nice homes northeast of downtown before returning to camp. Up was right. It was uphill for several blocks. We decided that bike riding, especially uphill, on my day off was too much like a busman's holiday. Anyway, the houses we did manage to see weren't that spectacular and it was hot – 90° hot.

The swimming pool back in camp felt good. We checked our e-mail, did some laundry and relaxed. It was exactly what we needed. The next day I planned to climb up Emigrant Canyon and start my assault on the Rockies. After Donner Summit in the Sierra and the many passes I had crossed in the state of Nevada, I felt confident. I was not expecting to lose quite as much sleep as I had the night before I crossed the Great Salt Lake Desert.

Our safe haven on the road: the motor home at twilight.

June 15 - Day 17
Salt Lake to Coalville
46.6 miles

I had difficulty finding Emigrant Canyon. After Nancy dropped me off, I rode north, then east and eventually managed to stumble onto a bike route. I spotted a bike rider turning onto my street and followed him uphill to the east. I brushed the southern edge of the University of Utah before I spied a second biker tearing down the street into town. I turned uphill, away from the city and soon entered Emigrant Canyon.

The Donner Party came down this canyon in 1846. Brigham Young and the Mormons came down a year later. Three or four miles up the canyon there was a marker that indicated to me that maybe the Mormons were a little better organized than the Donner Party. The Donner Party, who had reached this point on August 22nd, fought boulders and brush for four and a half miles. They gave up on the trail and decided to climb the south wall of the canyon, now called Donner Hill. They hooked virtually ever team of oxen to each of twenty-three wagons to accomplish this. It looked impossible to me.

The Mormon group battled to the same point, arriving on July 22nd, spent four hours cleaning up the rocks and brush in front of them and rolled into the valley of the Great Salt Lake. A few miles later Brigham made his historic "This is the place" statement, pointing out into the valley. A monument, overlooking the city, now marks the spot.

I noticed that the Donner Party was a over a month behind the Mormons. The Mormons were virtually at their destination, while the Donner Party still had to traverse the desert and all of Nevada. No wonder they were late crossing the Sierra Nevada. Comparing the two parties at this point in their trip, it seemed obvious to me that the Donner Party was either naive or badly led. I guess they could have just been incredibly unlucky.

The canyon was full of bike riders and they were all pretty strong. I was passed by two riders and, when a third caught up with me, I asked him what he knew about the route I had planned for this day – up Emigrant and then over Parleys Summit on I-80. He thought it sounded all right and asked me where I was headed. When I told him New York City, he glanced at the small amount of gear I was hauling. "My wife is following me in a motor home," I explained. He was modestly impressed with the fact that I was riding across the country and genuinely amazed that Nancy would agree to accompany me for the entire way. He was a tri-athlete and had just finished his swim workout. After riding with me for a few miles, he wished me good luck, pulled away and vanished up the canyon.

Emigrant Canyon, early gateway to Salt Lake for the Mormons and the Donner Party.

I passed a restaurant about eight miles out of the city. I wasn't hungry and didn't stop. There had been virtually nothing between towns when traveling in Nevada. I felt like I might have returned from the wilderness. Wildflowers were blooming, the stream was singing and I was enjoying my ride very much. The ride up Emigrant is one I'd recommend to anyone.

I reached the top of the canyon, a place called Little Mountain Summit, after a 12-mile climb. I felt good and dashed down the other side toward I-80 where I quickly ran into trouble. I found the freeway under construction, with no shoulder on the right side of the road for me to ride on. Nancy was still behind me. I could give her a call and have her carry me past this significant bottle neck. No sense risking life and limb. I looked across the highway and noticed that there was a row of large orange-colored barrels separating the traffic from the area of the road they were working on. Why not ride there? I waited for a break in the traffic and dashed across the three lanes to the other side to check it out. I was now separated from the traffic by the barrels and had my own bike path that was not only fifteen feet wide, but also newly paved.

Nine or ten miles later I reached Parleys Summit, just over 7,400 feet. The climb had been difficult, probably the steepest ascent I'd had so far. I no longer felt so great. I was hammered, and happy that this day was scheduled for only forty-seven miles. Nancy rewarded me with lunch at the top and I tried to recover before coasting five miles down the other side of the pass. I stopped there at the road to Park City, met Nancy again and loaded my bike onto the motor home for a little detour.

Park City was only five or six miles off our route and we wanted to check out the site of the 2002 Olympic Games. Like Aspen, Colorado, Park City was a booming mining town in the late 1800s. The city had preserved

many of the old downtown buildings and had a lot of charm. We walked Main Street, up one side and down the other. I still hadn't recovered from my climb and slowly shuffled along the sidewalks. With my stiff-legged, hobbling stride, people must have thought I was either injured or aged and arthritic. We entered an ice cream parlor and I dropped exhausted into a chair, leaving Nancy to order for both of us, too tired to even wait in line behind the single customer. After fifteen minutes in the chair and one large scoop of chocolate ice cream, I began to improve. I have always believed that chocolate ice cream has special magical medicinal qualities.

While visiting a small museum, we ran into a local boy who was browsing along with us. We finished the upstairs and went down to look into the old jail in the basement. A dungeon would have been a better name for the place that contained nothing but rock walls with old iron doors and barred windows. Our young friend pointed out that a couple of the windows had been filled in. "Why do you think they did that?" I asked. He knew.

"Well, they would put people in this jail if they had

Above: A marker for the California, Mormon and Pony Express Trails. Right: Park City, Utah, historic mining town and home of the 2002 Winter Olympics.

pulled off onto the old road, the Lincoln Highway, and rode through two small towns before arriving in Coalville, our destination. I was twenty minutes in front of Nancy for a change. She had shopped for food and looked in at the factory stores near Park City before following me down the hill.

Coalville had a beautiful campsite in a park next to a small stream so swollen with spring runoff, it was nearly overflowing. Large willow trees shaded the stream, their trailing branches dipping in the water, floating, pulled along in the direction of the current. It was easily the prettiest place we had spent the night. We unloaded the barbecue, the lawn chairs and table and dined outside.

June 16 - Day 18
Coalville to Evanston
41.7 miles

In the morning, I rode across the freeway from our camp on the river to town. The sun was hiding behind a few clouds and the temperature was in the mid-sixties. An old auto dealership was closed, but continued to display two very old Buicks in the front showroom. A 1909 calender was taped to the window. It seemed symbolic of the fact that this town hadn't changed all that much from the days when the Lincoln Highway brought the world down Coalville's Main Street. The "Merc," short for Mercantile, was another element of this time warp. It was an old fashioned grocery store and meat market with dry goods and hardware areas in large rooms out in the back. The store was a living history museum, a working example of the old time general store.

The next six miles were delightful and the riding was easy for a change. I was riding on the old road with virtually no traffic, a large reservoir on my left. A camp-

Top: An unusual store near Coalville.
Below: Nancy enjoys the beauty
of the Coalville campsite.

too much to drink – if they were drunk. One guy never seemed to get sober, even after he was in jail for a day or two. The jailers discovered that one of his friends had rigged up a hose to siphon alcohol to the drunk through the barred window. The sheriff put a stop to this by bricking up the windows in one of the cells."

After our visit, we returned to I-80. I unloaded the bike, rode back onto the freeway and headed north toward Wyoming. After ten miles, I

site and a resort, both on the lake, were filled with motor homes in anticipation of the big fishing derby coming up this weekend. The derby had been advertised on a large banner that spanned the width of Main Street. A deer startled me when it jumped up about twenty feet in front of me and bounded away into the mountains. Black birds assailed me six or seven different times. I was unsure why they thought I was such a threat. Perhaps they were just protecting their nesting areas. I could hear their cries and see their shadows as they dove at me, but they never made an actual strike, remaining behind me, out of my sight.

I turned north into Echo Canyon, still on old roads, and saw a state maintenance facility up ahead. The Stars and Stripes, flying from a tall flag pole near the road, was pointing directly at me – the chain clanking against the pole like a bell. Another head-wind. It wasn't a gale force wind but it was definitely a stiff breeze that made a flag fly straight out. I was beginning to feel like the Li'l Abner character who was always shown with a small rain cloud above his head, following him everywhere he went. Instead of a rain cloud over my head, I felt like I had a huge fan permanently fixed to the front of my bicycle creating a constant head wind.

Echo Canyon also signaled the return of the transcontinental railroad. The old highway I was on, snuggled, literally squeezed itself, between the double rail line and the high red rock cliffs of the west side of the canyon. Fortunately, this highway did not climb as steeply as the road over Parleys Summit the day before.

This road was the very same road I traveled by car with three high school classmates in August of 1960. A few months after high school graduation, four of us headed for California, following a route not that different from the one I was following now. We picked up a speeding ticket in Nebraska, visited a classmate working on a ranch in Wyoming, took a swim in the Great Salt Lake, did a little illegal gambling in Nevada, and visited Yosemite, San Francisco and Disneyland in California. After our visit to Disneyland one evening, we jumped in our car and crossed into Tijuana, Mexico, just after midnight, to sample night life south of the border.

By the way, Echo Canyon doesn't echo. It did collect the sound created by the big rigs that rolled along the Interstate a quarter mile away and funneled the noise over as a I continued my ascent. There didn't, however, appear to be any summit. I just continually followed the road up for thirty-five long miles onto the high plateau of Wyoming. Halfway up, I stopped for a short personal celebration. My two year old bike reached the 10,000 mile plateau. The last few miles near the top of the canyon were steep, but the climb was not the equal of the previous day's marathon. Nancy caught me about ten miles out of Evanston and provided some lunch and a foot massage.

I was tired and happy to be in Evanston. Seems like the end of the trail never looks too bad after you've been riding for a couple weeks. This railroad town in cowboy country is above 6,700 feet. It had a beautifully restored depot, an interesting downtown, a large rodeo yard and one of the best camps we've stayed in. At this high altitude, it was the height of spring. The trees had new leaves and lilacs were blooming all over town. You could not only see them, you could smell them. Nancy discovered Dave's Fine Meats and bought two of their finest steaks.

Above: The Lincoln Highway squeezes between the railroad and the rocky buttes in Echo Canyon. Below: The restored railroad depot in Evanston under a dramatic sky .

Though we travel the world over to find the beautiful,
we must carry it with us or we find it not.

—Ralph Waldo Emerson

Wyoming

June 17 - Day 19
Evanston to Lyman
44.7 miles

Thunderstorms blew through our camp during the night. I thought they would be gone by morning, but the sky still looked dark and threatening. I put on a long-sleeved jersey, but decided against the raincoat. A couple miles out of town I was questioning my decision to leave the raincoat behind. The freeway sloped upward to the east. So what else was new? Well, a nice tail wind was new! Where had that been for the last week?

Before I left in the morning, I studied our maps and Greg Franzwa's book on the Lincoln Highway in Wyoming. I had determined that just east of town there was a fifteen mile section of the old road that would take me off the freeway and away from the noise of the traffic. After I exited the Interstate the road surface looked a little rough, but the quiet was nice. A mile later I saw a sign that said "Pavement Ends." It looked like another mistake. The free-

way was still running alongside of me – above me, up a forty-foot embankment, and separated from me by a barbed wire fence. I didn't want to retreat, so I lifted my bike over the fence, crawled through after it, and then pushed or dragged the bike diagonally up the embankment the height of a four-story building. I arrived at the top, winded and ready to continue my journey.

I reached my first summit after eight miles and enjoyed a five mile bobsled ride down to the bottom. Up again for two or three miles slowly, and down again for three miles swiftly. One final climb of four miles brought me to my third and final summit of the day. The summits were all over 7,000 feet, but they were not as difficult as many of the other climbs I had made over the last couple weeks. As I headed down towards Fort Bridger, the tail wind that had

At left: Preparing for the day, studying maps at breakfast.
Above: The challenging summits of the Three Sisters just west of Ft. Bridger.
Facing page: I-80 climbs up a range of buttes east of Lyman, the magnificent Uinta Range to the south.

Above: Pony Express and Lincoln
Highway markers at Fort Bridger.
Below: Headstone for a special friend,
the dog Thornberg, who died in 1888.

Fort Bridger was a major stop on the Pony Express Trail and a stable used for their mounts still stands on the grounds. Few institutions in American history have generated as much interest or seized the imagination of the public like the Pony Express. This experiment in swift mail delivery began its first run on April 3, 1960 from St. Joseph, Missouri, the western terminus of the nation's railroad system at that time. Relays of men riding fast horses carried letters and small packages across 1,966 miles of prairies, mountains and deserts to Sacramento, California. This system could delivery a letter between these two cities in ten days or less. Previously mail traveled by stagecoach or boat and took more than three weeks to travel to California from the eastern portion of the country.

Bridger claimed he was "the true discoverer" of the Great Salt Lake. During the winter of 1925, he followed Bear River to a great shallow bay. He found the water salty when he tasted it and determined that he had come upon an arm of the Pacific Ocean. The following year four other trappers established once and for all that it was a saltwater lake. Bridger also discovered the South Pass of the Rocky Mountains and was one of the first white people to view the wonders of present day Yellowstone National Park.

I waited for Nancy in the old trading post inside the fort, staffed by a woman wearing a period costume. We started talking and she asked me how far I had ridden. "I came from Evanston today," I answered. She was impressed. "That should have been a hard ride. You had to cross the Three Sisters. That highway can be really treacherous in the winter. The crowns of the sisters can turn into sheets of ice. It's okay in the low areas, but the crests can be hairy. Winters are windy and the snow will drift high over the roads. That freeway can be shut down for two hours or as long as three days once a storm

been providing some help during the morning kicked into high gear. The countryside flashed by at thirty miles an hour. The road was maybe slightly downhill, and I was not even pedaling. If I could just retain these conditions, I could be in Cheyenne, 360 miles away, way ahead of schedule.

Fort Bridger was the spot where all the major roads west had converged, a major supply depot for the emigrants. In 1849 alone, twenty-five thousand gold seekers traveled overland on the California Trail to the foothills of the Sierra Nevada mountains, most of them young men without families. The Oregon Trail was the first major route to the west. It started carrying pioneers in 1841 and continued for thirty years. The Mormon Trail, the Overland Trail, the transcontinental railroad and the Lincoln Highway all passed by Fort Bridger. Jim Bridger built his fort in 1843. He was considered the king of the mountain men and his knowledge of the west and the trails across it was without equal. About 300,000 emigrants passed through this area, stopping by the fort to seek his advice, buy supplies or have repairs made to their wagons. One out of ten died on their trip west.

rolls in." I told her I grew up in Iowa and remembered waking up after a big blizzard, eating breakfast, and listening to the radio, waiting for the announcement that there would be no school in Garner that day. Our school district always seemed to be the last to admit defeat. When the announcement came, we would cheer and dash upstairs to get dressed so we could meet our friends to play in the snow.

I told her that I had come from San Francisco and was aiming for New York City, following the Lincoln Highway. "Did you have to ride up Parleys out of Salt Lake?" "Yeah, and it was no picnic. I thought it was the most difficult climb of the trip." "How long will it take you?" "About eight weeks, I hope." "How were you able to get that much time off work?" "I'm self-employed and decided to give myself the time off." She laughed and said, "That sounds fantastic! Running a couple marathons is the closest I've come to doing anything like that. The marathon in St. George, in southern Utah, is beautiful. My husband still runs two marathons a year, but I gave them up. They just wore me out." She wished me a safe trip.

Nancy arrived a few minutes later and I consumed two sandwiches for lunch made from last night's leftover steak. Breakfast had been twelve pancakes with syrup and butter, half an apple, a banana, and a glass of orange juice. Dinner, the night before, had been steak, baked potato, salad and broccoli. These were only the meals and do not include the snacks during the ride or after the ride or ice cream in the evening. It was definitely not the diet plate, but everything did taste fantastic. My body seemed to crave the calories. It needed fuel. One advantage of riding your bike across the country was that you can eat all you want.

We spent over an hour at Fort Bridger, Wyoming's most visited state park, touring the museum and walking around the grounds. I rode another hour, through Lyman, with the wind pushing me along. What a treat. I hoped it would stick around for a few days. The sky in the west was turning black when Nancy picked me up and we drove to the RV park for the night, the wind pushing the camper all over the road, rocking it from side to side. The sky got darker and a real storm seemed to be brewing. We got a few drops and a lot of wind, but that was it. I rode forty-five miles and, for the first time in recent memory, I didn't feel totally exhausted. Maybe I've turned the corner. Probably it was just the tail wind.

June 18 - Day 20
Lyman to Rock Springs
58.9 miles

A crystal clear morning with a bright blue sky, a warm sun and a spectacular view of the snow covered Uinta Range to the south. I climbed up over a range of buttes – steep umber cliffs of eroded rock facing the valley – riding on the wide shoulder of the Interstate. The range land was blanketed with dry sagebrush – a countryside of wide open spaces. The words of a song came to mind. *"Let me ride through the wide open county that I love. Don't fence me in."* My spirits were soaring.

Fifteen miles into my ride, I reached the junction of I-80 and US-30. I would now follow Highway 30, more or less, all the way to Philadelphia. The Lincoln Highway Association was disappointed in 1925 when they learned that the federal government had developed a numbering system for all the major highways in the country. The Association lobbied to have Highway 30 extend the entire length of the Lincoln Highway, across the country through Salt Lake and on to San Francisco. Instead the

Right: One of the dozens of billboards announcing Little America. Below: The Lincoln Highway sweeps along the Green River, past the Palisades and Tollgate Rock.

government stopped about 900 miles short and sent US-30 northwest through Idaho, into Oregon. In a triumph of efficiency over poetry, the Lincoln Highway ceased to exist. The same mistake was not made when the Interstate system was designed. I-80 closely followed the path of the Lincoln Highway from coast to coast.

The most dominant visual element in the first twenty miles was a series of billboards advertising Little America, a vast tourist and truck oasis. The billboards all featured a huge photo about ten feet wide and twelve feet high on the left side of the billboard and a message in the rectangular white space to the right.

> *Stake your claim on the range.* (picture of big steak)
> *Always in gear, 24 hour mechanic.*
> (immaculate mechanic holding tool)
> *Break for coffee – always open.* (giant cup of coffee)
> *Running on empty – 5 miles Little America.*
> (cherry pie)
> *A room with a view.* (swimming pool)
> *Get the picture – 31" TV in every room.* (huge TV)

I stopped at Little America, named after Admiral Byrd's discovery in the Antarctic, for a rest and a drink with Nancy. So did several dozen eighteen-wheelers. The land was not nearly so mountainous anymore. The climbs were shorter and not so steep and my speed and energy were up. In Green River, we had lunch in the motor home across the street from a new park. The road into town was spectacular. We came across the wide, powerful Green River and then along a series of rock formations on the north side of the road. First came a succession of high, undulating red buttes called the Palisades, then a massive castle-like formation called Tollgate Rock, and finally a progression of unusual formations high on the cliffs: the Towers, Eagle Rock and Giants Thumb. In 1869, a major expedition to explore the Grand Canyon led by John Wesley Powell left from an island in the Green River just a mile south of here.

Nancy picked me up on the east side of Rock Springs after a sixty mile ride. I didn't feel too bad, not limping, not exhausted. We spent a little over an hour poking around the town's antique shops. An old "Rock Springs Coal" sign that previously arched over the Lincoln Highway at the entrance to town had been relocated to a park next to the railroad in the downtown area. There was also a statue of a coal miner in the park, celebrating the men who had worked in the mines, the principal industry of the city, supplying coal to the many locomotives that traveled through here on their way across the country. I ended the day reviewing maps and reference material, working on the routes for the next few days.

The Rock Springs Coal sign.
Left: When it arched over the Lincoln Highway.
Right: As it appears today in a downtown park.

June 19 - Day 21
Rock Springs to Wamsutter
65.7 miles

In the morning, a few miles outside of Rock Springs, we stopped to visit the Point of Rocks stage station. It was in business between 1862 and 1869 until the operation was effectively killed by the new railroad. The railroad made the West more accessible, allowing a person to travel coast-to-coast in about a week. By contrast the overland stage took over 45 days. A journey via the Isthmus of Panama demanded roughly 35 days, and a voyage around Cape Horn required almost six months.

The station and stable were made of stone and had either survived amazingly well or had been carefully restored. The station had a dirt floor and a well-used stone fireplace. The accommodations were rustic, but must have been welcome to cross country passengers after a rough ride sitting in a dusty coach over miles of bad roads.

Nancy and I agreed to meet for lunch at a rest stop five miles up the road from the stage coach station, but a mile and a half before the rest stop, a sign appeared in front of me that read "Road Under Construction - Next 14 miles." All traffic from the two eastbound lanes was being diverted to one of the westbound lanes; there would be no shoulder for me to ride on anymore. Nancy, who was ahead of me, had found a place to pull off the road to wait and see if I needed any assistance. I pulled up next to her and we walked over to the eastbound lanes to see if I could ride on them. They looked fine and a center section was freshly paved with blacktop. I sailed along the eastbound side of the freeway on my own private bike path, arriving at the rest stop easily.

After lunch Nancy agreed to wait for forty-five minutes before setting off for Wamsutter, our destination for the evening. That would give me time to navigate the remaining twelve miles of the construction zone. If I had any problems, I could wait for her to come by and pick me up. The road on the east side of the rest stop had not been paved. A large grinder had chewed out several inches of blacktop leaving an extremely rough surface. It felt like I was riding on the top of a huge cheese grater. My speed was reduced, but I was managing to bumpity-bump along in safety.

Off to the south, a mile or so ahead of me, I noticed what appeared to be a rain storm. I hoped it was moving east, away from me, faster than I was moving along the bumpy road. I ignored it until I saw a flash of lighting off in the midst of the storm. I soon saw another flash and heard the crash of thunder about six seconds later. I attempted to rationalize my predicament by doing some quick calculations. At 1,100 feet per second, the speed of sound, I calculated that the storm was still over a mile away. No problem, but I definitely needed to devise a contingency plan. I felt a few scattered drops of rain, a sign that the storm wasn't far away after all. I watched for the lighting, counting the seconds until I heard the thunder. If the count was under five seconds, I needed to find shelter. Suddenly, a dazzling rope of lightning – bright against the dark clouds – shot through the sky off to my right. Soon I has hearing thunder be-

hind me as well. I was surrounded and realized I was in serious trouble. I needed to get off the road and find a safe haven. It began to rain and the wind started to blow, hard, right at me, further slowing my progress. I stopped to shove my phone and my small tape recorder into my rear bag in an attempt to keep them dry. Everything seemed to be going wrong on this fourteen mile piece of highway.

Up ahead, I saw a grove of trees on a hill and hoped it would be the refuge I was seeking. The crash of thunder was now all around me. I could almost feel energy collecting in a lake beneath my wheels, searching for a high point to discharge towards the angry heavens. I became increasingly concerned about the possibility of being struck by lightning and doubted that the narrow one-inch rubber tires I was riding on would be adequate to insulate me and my bike from the earth. Riding along in this vast, treeless expanse, I felt like a telephone pole – a tall, moving lightning rod.

I came to an exit, just before the trees on the hill, and decided to turn off my private bike path and seek shelter at a place called Table Rock. A short distance from

Road construction and afternoon storm clouds outside of Rock Springs.

the exit I found a small, combination service station, convenience store and bar. Now how could I notify Nancy, who, if she left on schedule, would still be some distance behind me? Our phones were not working in this remote location. I hoped she might see me making my way up to the store, but I was more concerned with just getting off the road. I was unprepared when she came driving up behind me, honking her horn. We arrived at the Turtle Rock store at nearly the same time.

I parked my bike and jumped into the motor home to wait out the storm and listen to Nancy's tale of rising panic during her search for me along the freeway. She had seen the lighting and left the rest stop early, hoping to rescue me from the storm. She drove along the freeway, in the construction zone, a prisoner in bumper-to-bumper traffic, trying to locate me off to her right. "I couldn't find you. I saw several bright flashes of lighting. Then there seemed to be lighting everywhere, and it was raining hard. I wondered where you were and I really got worried. When I saw the Turtle Rock exit sign, I pulled off to see if you might have been smart enough to get off the road. I was relieved to see you pulling up to the store." The thunder stopped after half an hour, but it continued to rain, pinging against the aluminum top.

I returned to the road and watched a streamlined, yellow-gold locomotive roll by. Red lettering along the side spelled out Union Pacific. Seldom did an hour go by without one of the determined locomotives passing in the distance, solemnly pulling its load along the rails. I found them particularly majestic now, highlighted in the afternoon sun, with dark storm clouds still visible to the east behind them. They announced their presence at crossroads occupied by mere automobiles with an arrogant blast from the diesel's horn.

In Wamsutter, we checked into a motel. There were no RV parks. The motel's name was spelled out in capi-

A Union Pacific train speeds by in the golden afternoon light.

Above: Snow fence waiting for winter. Facing page: The Continental Divide, a major milestone on the journey, and the Lincoln Highway monument to Henry Joy, who realized the dream of a coast-to-coast highway.

lishments. This was a cafe. The sign was accurate. It served good food.

When it's springtime in the Rockies. . . It was a great time to be in this part of the country, riding a bike or doing anything. Wildflowers were blooming in a sea of new green grass, cattle grazed near the road under cloudless blue skies, empty of any evidence of recent storms, and a nice tail wind was pushing me up Cherokee Hill. The tasseled heads of the long grass beside the road were nodding in the wind, bending toward the east, pointing my way. I spotted a pronghorn antelope looking at me from across the freeway. I stopped, pulled out my camera and attempted to move a few yards up the road for a better shot. The pronghorn watched me closely, and before I finished moving, the animal spooked. Instantly it was gone, the white patch on its rear signaling his departure. Meriwether Lewis described the animal as *"extreemly shye and watchfull insomuch that we had been unable to get a shot at them."* He was amazed by *"the rapidity of their flight. . . . It appeared reather the rapid flight of birds than the motion of quadrupeds. I think I can safely venture the asscertion that the speed of this anamal is equal if not superior to that of the finest blooded courser."*

Long lines of wooden snow fences were not finding much purpose this morning, but they did indicate that this country was not always so hospitable. A guy in a white Mazda whizzed past and gave me a honk, his arm extended through his sun roof, his fingers flashing me the V sign. Must have been another biker.

A few days ago I noticed what I thought were ground squirrels diving into burrows as I rode past. I rode up on three of them, just ten or twelve feet off the pavement. They were unaware of my approach. Two of them were standing on their rear feet, like soldiers at attention, backs straight, gazing intently off into the distance

tal letters: "MOTEL." It cost only $35, but I thought it overpriced. It appeared to be, however, significantly better than the other motel in town that consisted of five boxlike units sitting next to the road. We had dinner in a cafe located a block away. A guy sitting in the booth next to us wore a cap with the words "High Tech Redneck" emblazoned on the front.

June 20 - Day 22
Wamsutter to Rawlins
56.5 miles

I started the morning with another visit to the cafe next door. There was a sign above the building reading "CAFE - Good Food." It was obvious that people around here didn't believe in cute names for their estab-

away from me. With that characteristic pose, I knew immediately they were prairie dogs. Since then, I have seen them everywhere as I moved through the countryside. They warn each other of my arrival with a series of five or six quick high pitched peeps. When I first heard the noise, it sounded more like a cheep and I attributed it to birds. If I surprised them, they would give out a long squeal, followed by a couple of quick peeps, and dive back into their holes like they were shot out of cannons. They were a constant source of entertainment, peeping as I approached and scurrying for cover.

In 1804, Meriwether Lewis wrote in his journal about seeing "infinite numbers" of animals. Scientists have estimated that there were as many as five billion prairie dogs occupying million of acres of prairie in the late 1800s. A professor from Northern Arizona described the linguistic talents of the prairie dogs in a *National Geographic* article: "They possess the most sophisticated natural animal language so far decoded." He researched the alarm calls of one species and found that they discriminated among predators – humans, hawks, coyotes, and dogs. Moreover, the prairie dogs distinguished between people of different sizes, and they also gave the same call for a man after not seeing him for two months. "That blew me away," said the researcher. (I guess I was hearing the alarm call for tall cyclists.)

After eleven miles I reached the top of Cherokee Hill at an elevation of just under 7,200 feet. Back in Iowa they wouldn't call that a hill. Here in Wyoming, with the Grand Tetons soaring to over 14,000 feet, I guess they might consider this merely a hill. Anyway, it brought me to the Continental Divide, the backbone of the nation. (I actually crossed the divide three times, once the day before and twice during the morning.) This spot was the highest of the three and featured a major Lincoln Highway landmark, the memorial to Henry B. Joy, presi-

dent of the Packard Motor Car Company and the first president of the Lincoln Highway Association. He saw realized the dream of a continuous improved highway from the Atlantic to the Pacific. At the top of the monument is a quotation of his. *"That there should be a Lincoln Highway across this country is the important thing."*

Greg Franzwa, in his book on the Lincoln Highway in Wyoming, writes that Henry Joy camped at that spot in 1916 and witnessed the most spectacular sunset of his life. Franzwa also learned that Joy wanted to be buried on that spot and goes on to say, *"That didn't happen, but his widow, Helen Joy, had this tribute erected for him in July 1939. In 1915 his new Twin Six would have been purring along the 1913 route, alongside the railroad about two miles south of here. Joy, Austin Bement, and possibly another companion, were on their way to the Panama-Pacific Exposition in San Francisco. When Joy*

arrived, he refused to let anyone wash the big Packard Phaeton. He thought it would draw more attention if people could see the mud from all twelve Lincoln Highway states. He was right – it was one of the most popular exhibits in the Transportation Building."

My grandfather drove Packards and would trade his old one in every few years for a new one. He thought they were the finest automobiles made. I remember one that had a hydraulic leveling system. When an eight year old boy sat on the front fender, a motor automatically started and raised the front of the car. When I jumped off, the motor moved the front of the car back down a level. I loved that car and my grandfather never seemed to mind that his oldest grandson was playing on his new Packard. He was quite a guy.

So was my dad. When I was about two, my dad arranged an adventure for me, my first semi-independent cross-country trip. He walked with me from his store, Roe's Super Valu grocery, past Houdak's pool hall and Cropley and Kern's gas station to US Highway 18, which at that time, ran right through the middle of Garner, Iowa. He flagged down an old car driven by a farmer from Corwith and asked him if he would mind taking me over to visit my grandfather at the post office in Britt

The grim rock walls of the old Wyoming State Prison in Rawlins.

ten miles away. My grandfather was the postmaster. The farmer agreed and I was on my way. My dad then called my grandfather to warn him that I was coming for a visit. He was not too pleased with my dad's plan, trusting his grandson to a stranger, but I arrived safely and have enjoyed traveling ever since.

Wyoming is the birthplace or source for three of the principal river systems in the United States. The first is the Mississippi (through the Missouri, and its branches, the Madison, Gallitan and Yellowstone). The second is the Columbia (flowing into the north Pacific through its longest branch, the Snake), and the third is the Colorado River (by its longest branch, the Green). Reaching the divide signaled that I was nearing the end of this segment of the ride – a segment featuring the mountains and deserts of the west. It had been an adventure and a challenge, to say the least, but I was ready to reach Cheyenne and sample another, I hoped, less difficult section of the country, a section with towns more closely spaced and roads less severely inclined. Even though it was far too early for me to start thinking about the Atlantic, the streams and rivers that I crossed from now on would be flowing toward that eastern ocean.

I met Nancy for lunch in downtown Rawlins. She was parked a block away from the old railroad station.

After lunch we wandered into an amazing old bar – its walls covered with animal heads and antiques. The place had character and I would have liked to stay, have a beer and learn a bit about the town from the few locals that were assembled on stools in front of the long bar. I walked out, reluctantly, aware that I still had to ride for another hour. We looked in the window of a barbershop that had one wall covered with Wyoming license plates and another that featured a few pronghorn antelope heads and fifteen or twenty antique razors. It was Sunday and the barber shop was closed, but an antique shop was open. We found a few items that we couldn't pass up: an old Japanese sake container for Whitney's apartment in New York and a carnival chalkware kewpie doll for Nancy's collection.

Later we visited the old Wyoming State Prison, built in 1890. It continued in operation until about 1982. It was a grim place, much worse than I would have imagined. It was hard to believe that fifteen years ago, this place was filled with over 500 men. We saw the cell blocks, including maximum security, the cafeteria, the gym, the library, the hospital and death row. In the building that contained death row, there was a gas chamber where five men had died. I am not normally squeamish, but this place made me queasy.

We had a great guide who told some interesting stories. I particularly liked the story of Abbott the Rabbit. The Rabbit managed to saw his way through an iron bar that locked his cell door using wool yarn and an abrasive toothpaste. It allowed him to sneak out of his cell at night, not to escape, but to steal cigarettes and candy out of the commissary. The guards didn't discover this for over a month when an inventory turned up shortages in the store. As punishment, they threw Abbott the Rabbit was put in the "hole." The rabbit and hole bit didn't impress me as much as cutting through iron with

toothpaste and wool.

Thunderstorms were threatening again when we left the prison and I still had an hour to go on my bike. I jumped aboard and headed east to Sinclair, flying before the storm with a huge tail wind. Traveling along between 25 and 30 mph, I waved at a tandem bike and two other cyclists headed west, struggling against the wind. All were heavily loaded and must have been traveling cross-country. Sinclair was a company town, originally called Parco, the acronym for Producers and Refiners Corporation. Sinclair Petroleum acquired the refinery, as well as the town, in 1943 from PARCO, who founded the town in 1922. The old Parco Inn, located on the town square, was on the old Lincoln Highway. The mission-style hotel was closed, but it must have been a rare, impressive establishment – a wonderful place to spend the night before the Interstate came along. We peeked through the dusty windows at the hotel barbershop and cafe. I could imagine customers sitting in the barber chairs and filling the stools at the cafe's counter. I walked around to the back and looked into the ballroom, where a majestic fireplace provided the focal point. It was a good Father's Day – a call from my daughter and my son. That night I showered myself and bathed my bike.

Two old photos of the Parco Inn,
a impressive mission-style hotel
on the old Lincoln Highway.
Courtesy of Wyoming State Archives

June 21 - Day 23
Rawlins to Laramie
83.1 miles

The antelope appeared suddenly, running along next to the fence, just thirty feet away from where I was riding. I wasn't sure where it had come from, but it was now sprinting just ahead of me, looking for a way to escape. I was preventing it from fleeing towards the highway. It turned and looked at me as I kept pace on my bike, glancing at the fence and making a weak attempt to push through. The barrier must have appeared too solid and, thwarted, the antelope was forced to continue running away from me. There were several more looks and more attempts to find a way through the fence. Then the animal panicked and just exploded into the fence. Fur flew everywhere and I was sure it would be caught there, hung up in the wire. Instead, it pushed over the woven wire that comprised the lower half of the fence and under the lowest strand of barbed wire to escape into the field on the other side. The pronghorn must have been molting, losing its winter coat. There was no other explanation I could think of for the tremendous pile of fur that was left next to the fence.

Laramie was eighty-five miles away and I was looking for an easy day, a minimum of climbing and a maximum of wind at my back. A long day to Laramie and a fifty mile day to Cheyenne and I would be over the Rockies and out of the mountains of the west. I was yearning for some flatter land. I may have been looking too far ahead, because the first seventeen miles of my ride were nearly all uphill. Elk Mountain, off to the south, was 11,115 feet high. It reminded me that I still had a few more mountains to climb. Another song crept into my brain as I rode along.

"Home, home on the range, where the deer and the antelope play. Where seldom is heard, a discouraging word, and the skies are not cloudy all day."

I was definitely on the range, not a tree in sight, only cattle and an occasional antelope, but now the skies were cloudy and I had been uttering several discouraging words on the first long climb. It was cool and overcast, very different from the weather I'd experienced on my trip so far. Blackbirds continued to ride herd on me. Anywhere from one to half a dozen would follow along, trying to get me to evacuate their territory.

Wildflowers were blooming, creating rivers and ponds of blue flowers along the highway. One field was full of blue iris; other meadows were decorated with ribbons of yellow and flashes of red and white.

Aspen, Colorado, where I worked three summers while in college, is at 8,000 feet. I remembered the almost daily afternoon thunderstorms. The black clouds in front of me, in this high country, suggested that there was more than a possibility that I'd get wet this afternoon. The morning had been dry and I met Nancy for lunch in a rest stop about halfway to Laramie. I was tired. I felt like I had been climbing all morning. Even the occasional downhill had been against the wind. It appeared that the mountains of Wyoming were not going to allow me to leave easily.

Nancy and I agreed to meet one more time at an exit twelve miles ahead before she left me on my own and continued on into town. The sky had grown darker during lunch, but there was no rain in our area. Soon after I started riding again, lightning appeared in the distance, followed by the rolling crash of thunder. It started to rain and the wind picked up. It wasn't too bad and I rode through a shower, and back onto a dry highway. I still had about seven miles to go to the exit when I received a call from Nancy. She had just driven through a big storm and wanted to know if I was all right. I assured her that it wasn't raining where I was and that the pavement was dry.

Five minutes later that all changed. Something hit me on my right shoulder. It felt like someone had thrown a small rock at me. Soon I could see large drops making splotches on the highway. "Big drops," I thought, "to sting like that." Another drop hit my left hand and I could see a small residue of ice. I smiled and thought, "I might even get some snow." The temperature had dropped from the seventies down to fifty-five since lunch. Before I completed the thought, hail began to fall, slowly at first and then in earnest. It crashed off my helmet, pinged against my aluminium bike, bounced off the road and pelted me on my arms and legs. Ouch! This was not good! Suddenly the motor home magically appeared and pulled off the road in front of me. I leaped off the bike – rescued again by Nancy.

We parked on the shoulder of the Interstate, an area reserved for emergency parking. Trucks would rock the home from side to side when they rushed by, just a few feet away. We waited for the storm to pass. Twenty minutes later there appeared to be a break, and I put on my rain coat and headed for the exit about five miles away. A few minutes later it started to rain again and, before long, it was pouring. I actually enjoyed the ride. A rush of adrenaline had revived me and I rode vigorously into the storm. Trucks splashed by leaving clouds of mist in their wakes. I felt in touch with those early pioneers who crossed these mountains, walking, without benefit of motor home, a hundred and fifty years ago. I made the exit, shoes and gloves soaked, and rode up with a smile on my face to where Nancy was waiting. I gave her a loud war cry of celebration.

Another wait for the rain to clear and we decided to meet a second time at an exit about twenty miles from Laramie. A few drops fell during this next ride, but the problem now was not the rain. It was the wind and the continuous climbing. I was able to head down occasionally, but those periods seemed to only last for a few minutes and then I'd be headed back up again. A coyote walked across the freeway in front of me. As I came abreast, it glanced back at me and then loped up a little draw away from me. A few miles later, I collapsed into the chair of the motor home, sixty-three miles completed, twenty to go. I had some refreshment and a rest and was back on the road.

I came over a summit a few miles later. The Laramie Valley, at an altitude of 7,250 feet, finally stretched out below me. What should have been an easy ride into town wasn't – the Wyoming wind again in my face. I was reminded of the scene in the movie, *The English Patient*, when Ralph Fiennes is trapped in the cab of a truck with Kristen Scott Thomas during a sandstorm. Ralph's character describes all the exotic names the people of the desert have for the many different winds: the *giblee* from Tunis – that produced a rather serious nervous condition, the *azez* – a whirlwind from southern Morocco, and the *samoon* – a red wind called the "sea of darkness" by mariners because of the red dust it carried aloft. I had a few of my own names for the wind that was keeping me away from Laramie. A few miles out of town, a herd of seven pronghorn antelope ran along parallel to me for a few seconds, then turning in unison, and racing away like a flock of soaring birds.

As the exit to camp appeared in front of me, I thought about the day. It seemed like I had just passed my final exam, a last test administered by the mountains of the west – a test to find if could survive long distances, high altitudes, head winds, rain and even hail, all combined in one grand day. I survived the day, barely, and hoped, since it hadn't killed me, it would make me strong.

An original Lincoln Highway marker at the State Historical Museum in Laramie.

June 22 - Day 24
Laramie
Rest Day

Laramie was a good place to take a day off, a college town that reminded us of home. The University of Wyoming with 10,000 students provides a large percentage of a city's population of 28,000. We browsed through galleries, book stores and antique shops in the old downtown next to the railroad tracks, talking with many

Left: Downton Laramie.
Right: A statue of the
University of Wyoming
Cowboy.

friendly people, and making a purchase or two.

An elaborate old mansion – formerly owned by Edward Ivinson, early Laramie's leading citizen – housed the Laramie Plains Museum. Ivinson had purchased the city block from the Union Pacific Railroad for his home in 1870, when Laramie was only two years old. The home had been beautifully restored and was com-

pletely filled with furnishings from the early 1900s. Outside, I ran into a couple that were just getting off their motorcycle. I told them I had seen many motorcycles like theirs in town and asked them what was going on. They both smiled and said there was a convention in town for people who owned and drove these huge Yamaha Venture touring cycles. All the machines were brightly polished, with glistening chrome and shining paint. They had two seats, one behind and slightly above the other. This couple had driven from southern

Oregon. They pointed out that they were also members of CMA, the Christian Motorcycle Association, and wore hats and patches to display their affiliation. "We're pretty up front about that. Jesus is important in our lives. We also avoid wearing black leather because it tends to make you less approachable. People don't stereotype us if we just wear jeans." I would certainly not have confused them with Marlon Brando in *The Wild Bunch*. On this day, they were playing a bingo game that included visiting various Laramie landmarks to find numbers for their cards. We saw a sign that said B-7 at the museum.

The University was attractive with many old sandstone buildings in a park-like setting. There was a large, two-tiered football stadium and big, domed basketball arena. Wyoming, like many other states without professional sports teams, turns its loyalty to the state universities. The Cowboys of the U of W obviously attract large crowds to these sizable facilities, despite the fact that the biggest city, Cheyenne, only has a population of 60,000. Fraternity Row was set right across a park/intramural field from a line of sororities. We had prime rib sandwiches in a restaurant across the street from university. In Wyoming, we skipped the seafood on the menu and moved directly to the beef.

June 23 - Day 25
Laramie to Cheyenne
58.7 miles

I rode about five miles, from one side of town to the other, before pulling into the Village Inn and sitting down in a comfortable booth. The Ultimate Skillet Breakfast was prepared with potatoes, sliced mushrooms, diced ham, green peppers, tomatoes, onions and cheese and was topped with two large, grade-A eggs, two bacon strips and two sausage links. It came with either toast or three pancakes and I had my buttermilk pancakes with both butter and hot maple syrup. The coffee came with its own support system, or mothership, in the form of a insulated pitcher on my table. Normally after a breakfast this large, I would feel painfully full,

my stomach protruding over my belt, but I plowed through the entire breakfast without breaking stride, and didn't feel the least bit uncomfortable. I like Mark Twain's comment about breakfast, *"Nothing helps scenery like ham and eggs."*

Nancy was pleased the other day when she found gas for only 97¢ a gallon in Rawlins. It takes over 40 gallons of gas to fill the tank in the motor home. I felt like the motor home must have felt back in Rawlins, full of fuel and ready to conquer the canyon.

I left town, arrived at the Interstate and found that the gods were indeed smiling down on me. The wind was blowing vigorously out of the west. Since I had survived the many adversities these gods had subjected me to the day before, they evidently felt they could give me a break and assist me over this last barrier remaining in the Rockies. The road up Telephone Canyon, named after it was chosen in 1882 for the first telephone line over the mountains, was steep. It was only about six miles in length and the breeze created a wind tunnel between the canyon walls, urging me up Sherman Hill with every gust. It spite of the help, the trip up to 8,640 feet took me the better part of an hour. It was the highest point of my journey. The summit was marked by a towering monument to President Lincoln. The stone pyramid with an eight foot bronze head of Lincoln, soared upwards over twenty-five feet in three or four tiers.

While planning the trip, I had thought, "If I can only make it to the top of Sherman Summit near Cheyenne, I would have the Sierra Nevada, the deserts and the Rockies behind me." The sixty miles per day necessary to complete the journey to New York seemed not only possible, but probable as I gazed out to the east. I was about 8,000 feet above my next major goal, the Missouri River, and my confidence was high. I celebrated

The vista from near the top of Sherman Summit.

Capital Avenue in downtown Cheyenne during Frontier Days in the 1920s and today.

state behind. I didn't plan to return. I followed Happy Jack Road as it wound through some gorgeous high country. Around the first bend in the road there was a field of blue lupine that filled a meadow with color, extending like an alpine lake toward the mountains in the distance. I parked my bike, crawled through the barbed wire fence and wandered about in the field taking pictures. There were so many fragrant flowers you could smell them without bending down. Visions of Julie Andrews popped into my head singing, *"The hills are alive with the sound of music."* Ah, well, Julie's never around when you really need her.

The downhill runs were great but the wind was making things difficult. As long as I headed east I was fine. Unfortunately, the road continued to turn back and forth and the wind frequently blew from the side, almost pushing me over. Falling over would not be pleasant if I was standing still, but traveling at 35 or 40 miles per hour, it would be disastrous. I rode the brake, held on for dear life, and reached the entrance to Curt Gowdy State Park all in one piece. Nancy and I had lunch looking back at the mountains for the last time.

As the peaks receded in the distance, the land changed, opening up into a wide expanse of rolling grassy hills as far as I could see. There was an occasional tree near a ranch or in a drainage area, but, for the most part, the land was empty. I began to miss the mountains and knew that the scenery from now on would not be so spectacular. It would also get much hotter.

The railroad station in Cheyenne was a wonderful old stone building. They had recently finished renovated the exterior and were working on the inside. Nancy was waiting in the parking lot. I threw my bike on the back of the motor home and changed clothes before we went to the State Historical Museum and Archives. In the museum, as I was taking a picture of a sign from the

by posing for Nancy's camera on the monument, my bike raised triumphantly over my head. Two guys from Bulgaria were also taking pictures of us with their video camera. I wondered what they thought of our performance, until, after I climbed down, one of them climbed up to have his picture taken. They must have thought it was some strange American ritual.

I pedaled away from the summit and left the Inter-

Lincoln Highway, the director walked up. She asked me if I was interested in the highway and then directed me to the archives where they had several interesting old photos of the era that I copied.

After a short walk through the downtown, we ducked into the historic Plains Hotel lobby. Just beyond, we found the Wigwam Bar. It was a local watering hole and at six in the evening, it was a happy place. Everyone was having a good time, laughing and gesturing. We were among the few that didn't have a cigarette in our hands. In Davis, California, it's against the law to smoke within twenty feet of the entrance to a public place, let alone inside of one. We ordered two beers and relaxed, reviewing the day. Halfway through the beer, a man came by to see how we were doing. He was wearing a long sleeved plaid flannel shirt, jeans, a large belt buckle that depicted a ship at full sail, a black cowboy hat and boots. We told him what we were up to and he started to share some of his life history.

Charlie was born and raised in Cheyenne and spent twenty years on the rodeo circuit until he tired of the abuse his body was taking. His best events were bull-

dogging and bull riding, although he participated in all the events except calf roping. He spent the next twenty years in the Navy and claimed to have been in three wars: Viet Nam, Granada and the Gulf War. Hong Kong was his favorite port and, after he retired from the Navy, he started working for the railroad. "Double dipping," he said. His big disappointment was that Denver, a city of a million and a half, had enjoyed so much more prosperity than had Cheyenne, a city of 60,000. "We had the railroad, for Christ's sake, and all they had was some gold mining up in the mountains. The big difference was the politicians. Their politicians were able to convince the government to send everything to Denver."

A quick celebration on the Lincoln Monument at Sherman Summit, the high point of the trip at 8,640 feet.

Because our cash register receipt had a red star on it, we were entitled to an extra drink from the bar. I ordered a Fat Tire beer with a bicycle on the label in celebration of the day's accomplishments. My ride out to the camp was more demanding after consuming two beers, but I managed to stay on my bike.

To sweep down hills and plunge into valley hollows;
to cover as on wings the far stretches of the road ahead
and to find them in bloom as you approach.

—Alain Fournier

CHAPTER FIVE
Nebraska

June 24 - Day 26
Cheyenne to Kimball, Nebraska
64.8 miles

I didn't want to ride on the freeway, so I elected to follow a remnant of the Lincoln Highway. The decision turned out to be a real pain in the butt. I spent a considerable amount of time in the morning studying the route of the highway between Cheyenne and the Nebraska border. I guess I should have taken notes, because I soon found myself on a gravel road with a terrible washboard surface, bouncing up and down on my tender backside.

I was also lost. In desperation, I waved down a woman in a pickup to ask directions. She said it was at least five miles back to Highway 30, but thought that the road I was on would take me to Hillsdale. Hillsdale, I remembered, was one of the towns the old highway had passed through so I continued on. Main Street in Hillsdale had three old store buildings – all closed. I stopped to ask directions again from a man mowing his lawn. He directed me over more gravel roads to Pine Bluffs. Halfway there, the road appeared to cross the Union Pacific tracks. But, as I rode closer, I discovered that the on-grade crossing had been eliminated, the road

turning south toward the freeway. Since I trying to avoid the freeway, I pushed my bike through the weeds, carried it over the double tracks, through more weeds and back onto the gravel. With shoes and socks filled with stickers, I started again pedaling towards Nebraska. I should have stayed on the freeway.

Nancy met me for lunch in a park in Pine Bluffs, the last town in Wyoming. The town was located on the old Texas Trail, the route used by cattlemen to move their beef to Montana, made famous by the book and movie, *Lonesome Dove*. By mid-afternoon I felt like I was a thousand miles from Wyoming. I had exchanged the mountains, the wildflowers and the wild life of Wyoming for the waving grass and rolling hills of the high plains of Nebraska. The temperature was approaching 90°. It made me think of the cowboy's lament: *"Why-oh, why did I ever leave Wyoming? Why-oh, why did I ever have to go?"*

There was no paved shoulder on Highway 30, but traffic was light and cars passed me easily. Several times though there was the possibility that a car overtaking

Facing page: Curious cattle, a common sight in Nebraska.

me and one approaching from the other direction would arrive at the same time, leaving me with little choice but to stop and move off the road, out onto the grass. I never had to do it. Every single time, people slowed down, waited and then pulled out to pass me in the other lane. It was extraordinary. One time a man in a pickup coming towards me, slowed down, pulled off onto the grass shoulder, and stopped. This allowed a large truck to pass me that had been driving slowly behind me, waiting to get around. I waved to them both in appreciation; the man in the pickup waved back. No problem.

By the day's end I had ridden over 1,350 miles across our country, these United States of America, and had not experienced a single negative incident. The stories I'd heard of rednecks in pickups throwing beer bottles had just not taken place. If you listened to television news most nights, it would seem impossible for a defenseless cyclist to ride entirely across this country and survive. I had encountered thousands of people during the last three and a half weeks, in and out of cars, trucks and motor homes, and had been shown every courtesy. Riding cross-country had certainly allowed me to experience some beautiful scenery, but, more importantly, it had renewed my faith in my fellow man.

Kimball is the home of the High Plains Museum. Nancy called me on my cell phone and told me they had a case with Lincoln Highway artifacts and she would meet me there when she finished with the laundry. There were three boys standing in front when I rode up. The smallest one asked, "Are you going to ride that bike all the way to New York?" I told him I was going to try and I asked him if he knew where my wife was. "She's doing your laundry." I laughed and asked him if he knew where everybody in town was. "No, but she was here and told us what you two were doing." Bonnie, the director of the museum, was great. She showed us through every case, giving us the history of each piece. They had two exceptional quilts made by the wife of a man named Freeman. He was a member of Lincoln's Cabinet and the first person to use the Homestead Act to acquire free land in the nation.

It was easy to tell we were back in the Midwest. Everyone was friendly. Nancy said she was greeted by every person she passed in the grocery store and had several greetings turn into conversations. Nancy's doubts and concerns about our trip had nearly evaporated. She was relaxed and enjoying the journey. She was a great companion. She travels with curiosity and enthusiasm, makes friends easily, compromises when necessary and is tireless in pursuit of a new experience or treasure. She was also growing increasing accomplished behind the wheel of the twenty-four foot behemoth that had become a comfortable home for us.

We stopped for a beer at a local tavern registered on the national list of historic places. The interior had been used recently as the set for a beer commercial. There was a scrawny old fellow sitting next to us at the bar. He was seventy-six years old and only had a few teeth in his wrinkled face, below the most unruly shock of grey hair I had ever seen. He was wearing a red flannel shirt and bib overalls. Nancy ended up in a serious discussion with him, explaining how he could massage his feet to help the sciatic pain in his leg. They also exchanged remedies for arthritis. Nancy directed him to put two tennis balls in a sock and sit on them when he watched television. He suggested that Nancy use a special liniment that he was using to good effect. I watched the interaction with interest and have to say it all seemed a bit unreal. After over thirty years of marriage, she can still surprise me.

June 25 - Day 27
Kimball to Sidney
38.8 miles

Dix, Nebraska has a population of 229 people according to the sign at the edge of town and, if anything, it appeared to be exaggerating a bit. Dix is eight miles east of Kimball and exactly eight cars passed me as I rode between the two towns. The highway was back in its typical location between the railroad and the Interstate, just as it was when I left Davis over three weeks ago. The wail of the Union Pacific's diesel locomotives was more common now than the sound of the passing automobiles. I was surprised to see a group of oil wells pumping away, looking liking giant prehistoric chickens pecking at the ground for worms. I was unaware that western Nebraska had oil.

Eight miles later I arrived in Potter, where an ordinary day became remarkable. There was an antique store on the highway. I was hot and the wind was making my life miserable again, blowing powerfully from the south, so I didn't need much of an excuse to stop. I wandered through the store and ended up buying an old Nebraska license plate. I had collected plates from nine of the twelve states I would be traveling through. I told Fern, the owner of the store, what I was doing. She said, "You should go into town and talk to Dale. He runs the other antique shop and is really interested in the Lincoln Highway."

Dale Dedic is retired from IBM and lives once again in Potter, where he was born and raised, after spending thirty years in Boulder and Tucson. He runs the Chestnut Street Memory Station and is responsible for the Lincoln Highway signs I'd seen in the last few towns. He became excited as we talked about riding from coast to coast and thought that the newspaper in Sidney would be interested in talking with me. Then he said, "I want

to buy you a Tin Roof sundae. Just up the street at Potter Sundry, they invented that sundae. It was named after the pressed tin ceiling they have in the old building." How could I refuse? We walked over to Potter Sundry and Dale ordered the sundae for me, announcing to the group gathered there, "This guy is riding his bike all the way from San Francisco to New York City following the Lincoln Highway." Three women sitting in a booth across from us were full of questions. They laughed, shook their heads and said, "Oh, my!" several times. They all wished me well before they left and one of them patted me on the shoulder and told me to be careful.

The sundae was large, delicious and disappeared in ten minutes. Dale told me how eight small towns along Highway 30 were working together to improve their communities. He had proposed the project that resulted in the Lincoln Highway signs along the main streets and

A major storm brewing in the evening outside of Sidney.

Cabela's in Sidney.
Above: the display of North
American game animals at
the rear of the store.
Right: The central aisle of this
temple to hunting and fishing.

the development of a new brochure that chronicled the history of the highway in the eight towns. He was excited that several new houses in Potter had been built by people working for Cabela's, the big sporting goods store in Sidney. Potter, with a current population of 388, was actually growing a little. "You know, we should take a picture of you here in front of the store and we could have a Lincoln Highway article in our Potter monthly newspaper." He called the manager of the bank, who ran home to get a camera, and I posed for a picture.

I noticed a sign on the wall that illustrated that the folks in Potter had a sense of humor. It said, "You know you live in a small town when: you hear a dog barking and you know whose it is; the only time you need to lock your car is during zucchini season; and your area code is as large as the population."

I spent over an hour in Potter and enjoyed every minute of it. Back on the road east it was hot and windy, not a pleasant day for a bike ride. The wind was terrible, blowing hard out of the south, impeding my progress. About seven miles out of Sidney, I found Nancy waiting with a newspaper reporter. She had a camera and I was interviewed, sitting in the motor home, for the next day's paper. That was interesting, and two miles out of Sidney, I found another guy with a camera, taking pictures of me as I rode up. It seemed there were two newspapers in town. This fellow asked me to stop at the edge of town, talk to a second reporter and have another picture taken next to a 1928 Lincoln Highway marker. One day, three different newspapers. They weren't the New York Times or the Washington Post, but we all have to start somewhere.

In Sidney we had lunch and visited the Fort Sidney Museum, a frontier post that protected the builders of the railroad and the early travelers on the frontier trails that passed this way along the Platte River.

The other major attraction in Sidney was Cabela's, a temple to fishing, hunting and the outdoors. Right inside the entrance were two monumental bull elk, frozen in time, engaged in mortal combat, their massive racks of horn aimed at their opponent's flanks. The central sanctuary of this cathedral rises to a height of over thirty feet, with clerestory windows running the length of the central aisle. Your eye is drawn to the altar, a three-story exhibit of North American game animals at the back of the store, a hundred and fifty feet away. There were antelope and deer to the front of the exhibit, a huge moose, and an even bigger Alaskan brown bear on one side and, on a stone mountain in the rear were several big-horned sheep and mountain goats. Ducks and geese were suspended overhead in the traditional "V" formation. The right side of this "church" contained the "Shrine of the Colorful Creatures of Lakes and Streams," dedicated to the many denizens of the deep and the tackle and craft necessary to capture them. Hundreds of trophy fish decorating the walls. On the left, there was the "Horned Lords of the Open Range Chapel," consecrated to hunting, with a gun library, a huge selection of scopes and binoculars, an archery sector and dozens of antelope, deer and elk heads arrayed along the walls. In between and to the rear was an amazing collection of camping equipment and outdoor clothing. The devoted moved about this house of worship, paying homage with their Visa cards.

This day of oppressive heat, married to an ugly wind, gave birth, in the evening, to an angry dark sky. The manager of the camp assured me that the storm we saw brewing to the north was going to miss us and I put two steaks on the barbeque. I turned the steaks over once and, a few minutes later, heard it start to rain. Within seconds it had erupted into a powerful storm with sheets of water pelting the motor home and gusts of wind rocking it back and forth. I grabbed my raincoat and rushed out to rescue our dinner. I nearly drowned. I managed to turn off the gas at the grill and pick up the steaks, but discovered that I was unable to get back inside the motor home. The wind was blowing so hard I couldn't close the door! Nancy stood in the doorway laughing, totally out of control, at my predicament. She was unable or unwilling to help – even with the meat that I was only barely managing to balance in one hand. I finally made

Grain elevators are silhouetted against the sky at sunset.

it back inside, thoroughly soaked, but safe. I had to strip, towel off and put on dry clothes before I was able to eat dinner. We learned later that it rained two and a half inches in twenty minutes in the town of Gurley, just twelve miles north of where we were camped. There had been warnings of flash floods.

June 26 - Day 28
Sidney to Ogallala
68.3 miles

Only a few cars on the road today, so the main sounds were birds singing, the rustle and whisper of the wind rushing past my ears and an amazingly loud chorus of crickets, that continued to serenade me throughout the day. That wind, unfortunately, had moved to the northeast. It blew strongly, seemingly in an attempt to return all the air the powerful south wind had moved north the day before. Since I am constantly, almost continually, going east, the wind was a problem and it only became worse as the day progressed.

I postponed breakfast and made an early start, attempting to beat the heat and the wind. After seventeen miles I rode in to Lodgepole, my target town where I hoped to find a cafe. My first stop was Finch's Drug and Sundries, an old store, almost unchanged from the 1930s. A woman, who appeared to be seventy-five years old, was standing behind a marvelous soda fountain and three men were seated at the counter on stools drinking coffee. I asked about breakfast and was directed two blocks up the road to Judy's Country Inn. One of the men asked me what I was doing, so I sat down and ordered a cup of coffee. After ten minutes of conversation,

Below: The soda fountain at Finch's Drug and Sundries.
Right: A restored 1930 Ford with an original Lincoln Highway sign.

one of the men said he had to go and all three pulled a quarter out of their pocket, flipped them up in the air, caught them in their hands, and banged them on the counter. Frank, the guy in the middle had heads, the other two tails, so Frank was stuck with the check for the fourth day in a row. As I was leaving, I turned to the lady and said, "This is a really wonderful old store." She looked up, frowned, and said, "Well, it's all kinda falling apart. Can't find anybody to come in and clerk. It's just hard for me to keep up." I said I could sure understand and thanked her for the coffee.

My next stop was an old Chevrolet dealership that was now an automotive restoration shop. They had a gorgeous 1930 Ford coupe in the front window along with an original metal Lincoln Highway sign that would have been installed around a telephone pole. At the drug and sundry store, I had been told to walk around to the

side of the building to enter. When I did, I met the woman who owned the garage in partnership with her husband. She guided me through. In the back they were working on a 1956 Chrysler, a car she had been seeking for a long time. She told me this one was for her. The car had been stripped down to bare bones, no doors, windows or seats, but the radio in the dash worked. It was playing a big band song out of the forties, appropriately enough, and it sounded great.

Judy's Country Inn was busy, and I sat down at a long table across from an older fellow who was having a cup of coffee. Within five minutes we were joined by five other men, and five more cups of coffee. A few feet away, gathered around a table near the back of the cafe were seven women. Six family members sat at a third table. I did sort of stand out, wearing my tight black bike shorts and my bright Salsa Cycles jersey. I felt like one of those alien characters Han Solo encounters in the bar scene in the first *Star Wars* movie. All the men, except me, were dressed in jeans, blue work shirts and caps with names like John Deere, Chappell Cooperative Elevator or Pioneer Seed Corn printed on the crown. Two of them wore suspenders. The first topic of conversation, here and everywhere else in farm country, was the weather. "I got three-fourths of an inch of rain last night." "I didn't check my gauge this morning, but I got forty-hundredths night before last." "I've been getting anywhere from a quarter to a half nearly every week."

They commented on the size of my breakfast and I shared an Iowa story with them. "My friend, Leon Schimmel, grew up on a farm in northwest Iowa and they ate well, especially at harvest time. Breakfast included pork chops and potatoes, along with eggs, toast and bacon. They even served pie. Dinner, not lunch, was at noon and supper, not dinner, was in the evening. Both of these meals were bigger than breakfast. They

Amber waves of grain.

Below: The sentinel of the prairie, a grain elevator in Chappell and an old bank sign in Big Springs.

also had snacks, in the middle of the morning and the afternoon, where they ate sandwiches." One of the men remembered working hard and eating "really good" as well. "Every day, we got pretty darn dirty, sweating like crazy in that summer heat. Then we would all take baths – every Saturday night – whether we needed one or not!" Everyone laughed.

My Midwestern credentials established, we moved on to the crops. "You know, some of the wheat over by us is real golden yellow, almost ready for harvest, and other fields are still green." "I 'spect the fertilizer tends to hold those fields back some." One of the women came over. "I don't want to be nosy, but did you say you were from California?" I said, "I live in northern California, in a university town called Davis." "My daughter lives in San Francisco and she rides a bike. The other day, a Muni bus ran a red light, hit her and pushed her about seven or eight feet along the ground. Amazingly enough, she jumped right up and was just fine." I commented, "

I suppose San Francisco is not the best place to go for a bike ride, but I have sure had good luck riding through western Nebraska." I hated to leave, but I still had over fifty miles to go. Everyone wished me good luck and waved to me as I walked out the door.

I stopped in Chappell for a 25¢ glass of lemonade from a little girl that had a table set up next to the highway. She was having trouble with the change so I had a second glass and bought a 50¢ chocolate chip bar to make it an even dollar.

Nancy and I had lunch in Big Springs, the site of a major Lincoln Highway episode. The original route of the highway was to be as direct as possible between New York and San Francisco. Many cities that had been left off the route argued passionately why they should be included. Denver argued most ardently and effectively and, for a time, was on the route. Later, the highway was rerouted to the more direct, northern route, through Cheyenne. The Denver folks installed a large billboard at Big Springs, directing people to Colorado and Rocky Mountain National Park. The Lincoln Highway people installed their own billboard right next door. It was confusing enough traveling cross-country in 1915 without having to choose between competing roads.

At lunch, Nancy showed me copies of the *Sidney Telegraph* and the *Sidney Daily Sun* she had purchased before she left town. My picture was on the front page of both. Must of been a slow news day. The Sun's headline read, "Lincoln Highway leads man across U.S.," while the Telegraph's headline summed up its story with, "Bicyclist takes tour of U.S Highway 30." Both papers also featured stories about the big storm the previous night and the flooding that followed.

Shortly before ten in the evening, another violent thunderstorm descended, complete with high winds and hail. Rain fell in buckets and hail a half inch in diam-

eter beat a tattoo on the roof. We felt like we were trapped inside a large percussion instrument, right in the middle of a drum solo. Thunder crashed and the sky was bright with lightning every few seconds. The motor home rocked back and forth, each time a little farther, as it was buffeted by the wind. We turned the television to the weather channel and discovered that we were in the middle of a "severe thunderstorm area" and a tornado watch had been issued. Winds were reported at 67 miles per hour with gusts to 83. We were advised to go inside a sturdy building and stay away from the windows. Our structure, the motor home, was acting like a carnival midway thrill ride and we had windows virtually all around us. I was beginning to think that I would need some maps for the Yellow Brick Road. Kansas, where Dorothy had lived when she took an unexpected ride to Oz courtesy of a tornado, was only sixty miles to the south. I thought we might be airborne any minute. It was exciting at first, but as the storm grew more intense, it was scary. This trip had begun to resemble the old movie serial, *The Perils of Pauline*. We never knew what to expect next. Shortly after eleven the winds backed off a notch, but the rain and the lightning continued as we fell asleep.

June 27 - Day 29
Ogallala to North Platte
50.9 miles

On my way out of town, a flooded trailer park, located between the highway and the South Platte River, caught my attention. I stopped to talk with one of the residents who lived in the flooded area. He was out collecting night crawlers. For those unfortunate people who never had a chance when they were young to hunt this highly prized fishing bait, night crawlers are

worms about a quarter inch in diameter and six or more inches in length. On nights when rain flooded the night crawlers out of their holes, we took a flashlight, searched about in our back yard and picked up worms, easily filling a one gallon Folger's coffee can. I have no idea what we would have done with so many of the things. My mom probably threw them back into the garden the next day. See if you can visualize what a gallon of large, slimy worms would look like. Now, stick your hand down into them up to the elbow. Pure joy for a ten year old boy.

I was taking a picture of the flood when the resident said, "You should have seen this place an hour ago when the water was six inches higher. It was a really a sight. I saw a several blue gills over by that yellow trailer and a big old carp in that deepest part by the telephone pole." The deepest part was occupied by two kids who were having a wonderful time in the midst of this disaster, splashing and chasing each other in their new neighborhood pond.

Below: Kids in a flooded trailer park and a view of the Platte River Valley with the transcontinental railroad following the route of the pioneers.

Above: Interior of Ole's Big Game Steakhouse and Lounge. Right: An unusual welded construction with dozens of cowboy boots decorating a Sutherland front yard.

I was having difficulty remembering what day it was. In fact, I usually had no idea. Nancy informed me that it was Sunday; I thought it was Friday. Living in the present seemed to be a healthy way to exist.

As I traveled down the wide valley of the South Platte River, I could easily see why this corridor had been used as a passageway by generations of travelers headed west. The rolling hills to the north would have been much more difficult to traverse than this flat expanse next to the river. Present day I-80 and older arteries, like the Lincoln Highway and the Union Pacific Railroad, confirm just how superior this route has been and remains today. But on this day, my route would have been whole lot better if the wind hadn't continued to blow from the east.

In Paxton, I had a Coke in Ole's Big Game Steakhouse and Lounge. Rosser O. Herstedt, whom everyone called Ole, founded "Nebraska's favorite waterin' hole" the day after prohibition came to an end, August 8, 1933. Over a period of 35 years, he traveled and hunted all over the world, bringing back the 200 trophies and many photographs taken in the thirties and forties that filled the walls of his tavern. Ole's gone now and steakhouse is more of a family restaurant than a bar, or so it appeared on Sunday morning.

Nancy caught up with me for lunch in Sutherland, a town with several Lincoln Highway signs and two wonderful old gas stations, both closed many years ago. The first was tiny, a dollhouse with a gable roof and half-timber construction, the windows divided by mullions into panes about eight inches square. The second was a brick beauty with a tapered chimney in the front.

I rolled into camp in North Platte at what I thought was 2:30, but soon found that it was an hour later. We had moved into the central time zone thirty miles west of

town. Time zones were created in the United States thanks to the transcontinental railroad. Previously, towns had set their own time based on the sun. Back then, clocks, only a few miles apart, often disagreed. The four time zones that cross the "lower 48" were established in order to allow cross-country trains to operate on a schedule.

We had to hurry to visit the home of Buffalo Bill, located just two miles away. We toured the beautiful home he built in the late 1800s and enjoyed all the memorabilia, especially the posters from his Wild West Show. He named the place Scout's Rest Ranch and painted the name in large letters on the roof of his barn. He decorated the peak of the gables with an ace of spades with a hole in it, Annie Oakley's signature piece of sharp shooting in the Wild West Show. Bill would also give an ace of spades with a hole in it to friends. This could be used as a fee pass to the show. Bill was born in Iowa and

earned his nickname when he won a $500 bet by killing 68 buffalo in less than eight hours. His show put him in contact with celebrities and royalty all over the world, but his fame stemmed from the fact that he starred in a profusion of dime novels, comic books really, that were popular at the turn of the century.

Bill came west to ride for the Pony Express in 1860 when he was in his teens. Many of the riders were teenagers, primarily because lightweight riders were essential. A lighter rider meant that the horse could travel faster and stay fresher. Some 80 riders were hired to ride 400 fast horses. The young rider could also carry more mail at ten dollars an ounce in the specially-designed leather saddlebag. The saddlebag fit over the saddle, with only the weight of the rider to hold it in place. This design allowed the rider to move the bag from the tired horse to the fresh one in less than two

Left: Nancy stands in front of Bill Cody's house in North Platte. Above: An old poster from Buffalo Bill's Wild West Show.

minutes. The riders were paid between $100 and $150 per month.

During the summer of 1952, my parents, my sister and I took a trip west from Iowa. I was ten and had just finished the fourth grade. The trip also included a visit to a dude ranch in Rocky Mountain National Park, a chuck wagon dinner with several hundred others in the Garden of the Gods in Colorado Springs, the Cheyenne Frontier Days Rodeo, and the Black Hills with Mt. Rushmore. On our first day, we drove about 500 miles and spent the night in a motel with a swimming pool in North Platte, Nebraska. I remember that it seemed to take forever to drive 500 miles, sitting in the back seat, fighting with my sister and asking, "How much farther is it?" Now, nearly fifty years later, I was on another big trip and, once again, spending the night in North Platte, wondering how much farther I still had to go.

June 28 - Day 30
North Platte to Lexington
65.2 miles

It was warm and humid in the motor home when we went to bed and I opened the skylight, that was located directly over my bed to let in a little cooler air. It had showered briefly with some thunder and lightning, but it looked like we were going to get off easy that night. About two in the morning a huge crash of thunder woke me. Sheet lighting was illuminating the entire sky and the inside of our small home. Rain was pounding against the roof of the camper, sounding like we had parked under a waterfall. I turned over, attempted to go back to sleep and noticed that my thigh was cold and wet. Another huge flash of lightning turned my attention to the skylight above my bed. It was raining, pour-

ing really, through the hole in our roof onto my bed. I closed the vent, adjusted my cover so that the wet spot hung off the bed and just went back to sleep – the storm continuing into the night.

I was up early and rode into North Platte for breakfast. In the booth next to me, a couple was talking about the recent storms and the tornado warnings in the area. "You know, when the thunder gets so bad that it shakes the house, well, I just crawl under the bed," the woman said. "I don't blame you," her companion replied. "I went out and moved the pickup under a big tree to avoid the hail, but I was worried that a tree limb would fall on it." "Better a tree limb, than the hail," she answered. "I was out this morning picking up all the branches and lawn furniture that had blown all over the yard and I thought, what a mess. Then I thought of your cousins up north, that had everything ruined by the hail – the crops, the car, everything. She told me that there was six inches of hail on the ground when it was over." "I guess we were lucky after all," he remarked. I thought we all were.

I rode out of town, past the eight story Hotel Pawnee and the old Fox Theater; both had been landmarks in the middle of town for decades. Just east of town I rode across the North Platte River for the second time. The first time was in Wyoming, just outside of Rawlins. The confluence of the north and south forks of the Platte was only a mile away. Here the waters carried from the mountains of Colorado, near Denver, joined with those from a Wyoming section of the Rockies west of Laramie. I had been saving the word "confluence" for Pittsburgh, but I liked it so much I decided that I could use it twice on a cross country trip. Ft. McPhearson was just down river a few miles. Between 1863 and 1880 it protected workers and pioneers from the Indians. Bill Cody and George Armstrong Custer were frequent visitors.

As we left the sand hills of western Nebraska behind, the land to the north opened up with farmsteads and cultivated fields. Road signs pointed to towns both north and south of the highway, an indication that civilization extended beyond the immediate vicinity of the Platte River. Men driving pickup trucks in this part of Nebraska wore billed caps, not cowboy hats. They were farmers, not ranchers. The West was now officially behind us. We were in the Midwest with a new time zone and a new landscape to match.

Temperatures were in the high sixties, with a few, scattered, fast moving clouds and a lovely breeze, out of the northwest. A tail wind! I floated down the road, soaring, almost flying. A long Union Pacific freight train with five engines moved along on the north side of the road, actually creating a draft for me. I crossed the road, as close as possible to the train, to take better advantage of it, and was soon speeding along at over 25 miles per hour, just another car, pulled along by the long train.

With a tail wind, I moved along at about the same speed as the breeze. The sound the air normally made as it rumbled rushing past my ears was gone. I was traveling with the air, not through it. The sounds of the road were no longer concealed. Bird songs, a pond full of frogs, the whir of the bike chain and the noise of traffic coming up behind me was suddenly magnified. I felt like I was sitting on a back porch, relaxing in a comfortable chair, observing the pastoral scene, listening to the day.

The nearly seventy miles to Livingston passed easily. Nancy had caught up and joined me for lunch in Cozad. In Livingston we visited a few antique stores and I found some Lincoln Highway postcards to buy, but we were both still tired from our battle with last night's storm. We drove eight miles south of town to a lovely campground in a state park overlooking Johnson Lake. We parked our motor home in a grove of old maple trees just thirty yards from the shore. I finished my shower

Top: Sunset at Johnson Lake.
Above and right: An old Lincoln
Highway motor court in Cozad.

At right: The 1733 Ranch –
1733 miles east to Boston,
1733 miles west to San Francisco.
Opposite page: Photos of
Pioneer Village in Minden.

and soon had chicken cooking on the grill. While waiting for the sun to set, I looked out across the lake and crossed my fingers. I was hoping to avoid another storm during the night. What we didn't escape was the mosquitos. There were clouds of them, rising out of the grass, looking for their dinner.

June 29 - Day 31
Livingston to Grand Island
76.1 miles

It was quiet out by the lake, with no freeway or railroad nearby, and we ended up sleeping late. The morning was dark and overcast, and I was surprised to find that it was nearly eight o'clock when I finally rolled out of bed. We rushed through our morning routine. I had a bowl of cereal and we pulled away from our lake view location. We ran into rain before we arrived in town, so I took out my yellow rain coat and began to contemplate nearly eighty miles of bad weather, the distance that was lying between me and Grand Island.

It rained for a while and continued to shower through-out the morning, but that didn't turn out to be nearly as big a problem as the wind that had turned on me once again and was blowing out of the southeast. It was an ugly pig of a day, a gray-backed hog with a black snout sitting in the mud kind of morning, and I had a long way to ride. It was cold, 59°, not a hint of sunshine and a dull greyness as far as I could see in any direction. After a rain shower, it would lighten up a bit, gradually grow dark once more, and then shower again. I felt like I was going uphill. I wasn't, of course. The Platte River flows to the Missouri and the road I was on was either flat or heading slowly downhill. Having convinced my self of these truths, I began to contemplate my tires, which both appeared to be suddenly going soft – somehow losing air. I dismounted and examined both wheels and found absolutely no problem. The wind! Of course, it was the wind, dragging me down, causing my spirits to sag.

I began to feel better as I approached Kearney, despite the fact that it took me until just after noon to cover the thirty-six miles to get there. Just four miles before town, a historical marker proclaimed the former location of the 1733 Ranch, so named because it was exactly 1733 miles from both San Francisco and Boston. My calculations showed that I was 1610 miles from San Francisco and had about 1640 miles remaining until New York City for a total of 3250. Anyway, no matter whose figures you believed, I was about halfway there and that was good news.

Kearney was a great-looking town and the home to a branch of the University of Nebraska, the former Nebraska State Teachers College. You can't beat these great university towns. Living in one, as we do, may have something to do with my attitude. We toured the Museum of Nebraska Art, located in a handsome classical building just off the highway. They had a clay exhibition, with artists from around the nation. One of the artists was a friend of ours from California, Tony Natsoulas.

Nancy had visited a museum in Lexington while waiting to see if I would need to be rescued from a rain storm. She met Eileen Lauby, who was a teenager in Overton when the Lincoln Highway was first paved in her county. She remembers riding with her father, Nick Thinnes, and, as they drove onto the pavement from the gravel road, he said, "Now hold on, we're go-

ing on the race track!" He thought that traveling over twenty-five miles an hour was totally unnecessary.

I rode seven more miles east and met Nancy for a side trip to Pioneer Village, Nebraska's top tourist attraction, located fifteen miles south of our route in Minden. There were 10,000 items in the first building alone, featuring transportation, guns and money. I was interested in the cars from around 1915, the cars that would have been used on the first trips across the Lincoln Highway. I was immediately struck by the fact that these cars did not have any side windows, just curtains. They were little more than motorized covered wagons, despite their windshields and headlights. The roads at that time were terrible, and there were vast stretches of the highway that had no services of any kind. These early travelers had to camp, carry extra fuel and be their own mechanic.

In 1908, before the Lincoln Highway was built, an average Atlantic-to-Pacific auto trip took between sixty and ninety days. Henry Joy, who made several of those early cross-country trips, asked a Packard dealer in Omaha for directions to the road that went west out of town. "There isn't any," was the answer. Joy passed through fence after fence, following an early trail. After a few hundred miles, there were no fences or fields, just two parallel ruts running into the distance across the prairie. He found pieces of wagon wheels and other relics left by the many pioneers that had struggled along these trails around 1850.

Besides the museum or warehouse buildings, we visited many old structures that had been moved to the site from the surrounding area – an old schoolhouse, fort, frontier store, land office, sod house, church, firehouse, depot, pony express station, barn, and a variety

of farm buildings, all authentically furnished. We were overwhelmed during our too-brief two-hour stop.

We returned to Highway 30 and I still had 35 miles to go until Grand Island. As you leave Kearney, the road bends a bit to the north and the south wind that had been a thorn in my side all morning was now somewhat positive. My speed increased, my effort decreased and I started feeling that life wasn't all that bad. The sun came out and the temperature soared to 73°. Gibbon, Shelton, Wood River, and Alda rolled by. Wood River bragged that it was the home of Scott Frost, a star Nebraska quarterback a few years ago. I passed a huge Union Pacific construction project that continued for five miles. There must have been over fifty pieces of machinery, all fitted with both rubber and steel wheels so they could either ride the rails or drive on the roads. They were moving busily back and forth over the tracks, pushing, shoving and digging. In Alda I passed a bar that was advertising a Monday night special, dollar tacos. Three or four of those and a couple of beers would have tasted pretty good about then. But I pushed on. It was after 6:30 before I arrived in town.

June 30 - Day 32
Grand Island to Columbus
70.6 miles

Another slow start to the morning because I decided to visit the Stuhr Museum of the Prairie Pioneer in Grand Island before starting down the road. There was a exhibit spotlighting the 300,000 to 500,000 emigrants that made the journey west. The average cost for a family of four was about $600 plus an additional $600 to purchase goods when they arrived out west. This typical family would travel ten to twelve miles a day and spend five or six months on the trail. My sixty miles a day suddenly seemed like racing across the country, but the $600 they spent for their entire journey would only cover about a week of my relatively modest budget.

By 1870 the railroad had replaced the covered wagon as a method of transportation for pioneers traveling west. A settler could travel from New York to Omaha for a fare of $35, with a scheduled time of seventy hours. Another way to acquire land in Nebraska was to buy it from the Union Pacific which owned several million acres in the Platte valley.

A want ad on April 18, 1894 in the *Grand Island Independent* read, "Wanted, at once, good steady girl or middle aged woman for light work. German preferred." Grand Island was a town with a large German community. They had social clubs where everyone would speak German, enjoy German dances and sing German songs. During World War I, it all ended. I remember a township in Iowa, where I grew up, that changed its name from German to Liberty during those years.

Back on my bike, I found a cool day with high overcast. Just outside of town there was an original piece of the Lincoln Highway lying abandoned behind a gas station. It was significant because it was one of the original "seedling miles." When the highway was being developed, the board of directors collected money from the major players in the auto industry, and even had a campaign to raise money from the general public. Many of these dollars went to the states to build a mile long, paved section of highway, usually close to a town. Then people could come out from town and drive on the new road. They could see what they were missing and, it was hoped, be encouraged to find ways to continue improving other stretches of the highway in their area.

One small town was beginning to look very much

Above: The beautifully restored
Southern Pacific Railroad Depot
in Davis, California.
Left: The Palace of Fine Arts
in San Francisco, the only remaining
building from the Panana-Pacific
Exhibition of 1915.

Left: A derelict car in Middlegate, Nevada, a sight often encountered on the road.
Below left: Another reminder of a time gone by, a deteriorating barn in Pennsylvania still sporting an old advertisement.
Below right: A beautiful barn with pressed tin siding in Nebraska.

Right: Thousands of riders come from all over the world to take part in Iowa's RAGBRAI. On this annual ride across the state, the festive atmosphere and friendly people make this event unique.
Below left: The action is lively at this horse show in North Platte.
Below right: Gorgeous scenery in the Wasatch Mountains east of Salt Lake is typical in the spring.

Far left: Spring time at Iowa State University in Ames, Iowa. The Memorial Union is reflected in the waters of Lake Laverne.
Above: The magnificently preserved Union Pacific Depot in Cheyenne, Wyoming.
Left: The flower-filled meadows seem to go on forever in the mountains east of Laramie.

*Above: Diners of every description can be found
along the route of the old Lincoln Highway.
Left: Metal advertising signs make colorful
decorations in Belle Plain, Iowa.*

Signs of the times: signs of every description call your attention to gas, food and lodging. Below: Original Lincoln Highway markers still point the way.

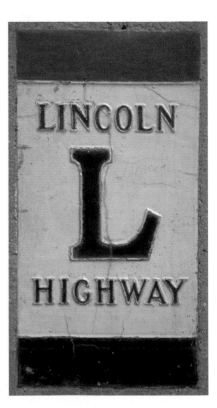

Motels all across the country competed with each other using flashy, eye-catching signs to entice overnight guests.

Clockwise from upper left:
The steel, stone and glass towers of Manhattan.
South Street, a colorful neighborhood in Philadelphia.
A relieved pose at the end of my journey,
The Coney Island Diner in Mansfield, Ohio.

like the last. Each had its own prairie skyscraper, the grain elevator, the sentinels that became beacons to me as I struggled along the road, searching for a sign that I was making some progress. Just before I arrived in Central City, where Nancy had agreed to meet me for lunch, it began to sprinkle. After lunch, I put on my raincoat and rode away in a light rain.

It wasn't long before it began to rain in earnest. There wasn't any thunder or lightning and the winds were modest, but I was getting wet. After about fifteen miles I caught up to Nancy and took a break, hoping the rain might stop. It didn't. I drug myself back into the rain and onto the bike, worried that it would get dark if I delayed any longer. It began to rain harder, blowing in from the south. My shoes, socks, shorts and gloves were soon soaked and water began to run down the lenses of my dark glasses. Spray from the passing vehicles enveloped me with clouds of mist. It was 60° and I was only managing to keep warm by continuing to turn the pedals. Well, at least I no longer thought the day was boring.

Twenty miles later, I stopped again and took refuge again in the motor home. My hands felt paralyzed – stiff and cold from holding onto the handle bars. I could hardly move my crippled fingers or even feel them. I towel dried my head, put on a sweatshirt and tried to warm up, thinking already of the hot shower that was only six or seven miles away. I took off my shoes, found a dry pair of socks and gradually began to feel human again.

The last stretch was easy. The rain stopped, the skies cleared and the sun came out. The New World Inn in Columbus had a room for us with two beds, a hot shower, a television and a telephone where we could check our e-mail. It looked pretty good. We dined downtown at Dusters. Nancy, hungry for seafood, decided on the "fresh" salmon. It was, however, raised on a nearby Nebraska farm. It wasn't terrible, just bland and taste-

Left: An old post card view of the Metropolitan Hotel in Grand Island.
Right: A restaurant, gas and lodging sign in Grand Island.

less, and it didn't compare to its cousin that lives in the Pacific Ocean. We decided to stick to beef, pork and chicken for the next thousand miles or so. Full, tired and finally warm, I fell asleep with Nancy working at the computer.

Architectural detail from a Columbus auto dealership, now a restaurant.

July 1 - Day 33
Columbus to Missouri Valley, Iowa
88.6 miles

I rolled my bike out of the motel into the parking lot at seven into thick fog and a dripping, saturated, 60° morning. It looked like it had rained all night. Everything was wet, including my shoes and gloves from the downpour I rode through the day before. My shorts, that I washed last night, were also still damp. I finished getting ready inside the motor home. A group of former University of Nebraska football players were up, standing around outside the motel, getting ready to play in a university golf tournament in Columbus. One of the men

hollered good morning to a guy named Bernie, who was pulling his golf clubs out of his car.

"Good morning to you," Bernie hollered back. "Getting up this early in the morning feels a little too much like those two-a-day practices we had to endure." He drove an impressive-looking, Cornhusker-red Hummer that was parked right next to me.

"What's with the weather, Bernie? Are we going to be able to play today?"

"It's going to burn off before too long," Bernie answered.

Bernie was right. By the time I finished my breakfast, the sun was out and I was on my way. The gutters along the road remained full and I was forced out into the traffic to avoid the deepest water. In this part of the country, livestock trucks seem to flow by in caravans, so I watched my rear view mirror carefully each time I took evasive action. By 8:30 the pavement was dry and I had to stop, take off my long sleeved jersey and put on sunscreen. To add to the growing good news, I found a friendly wind of significant strength at my back.

Not wanting to waste any of my good fortune, I pushed forward, stopping only briefly in each small town. Fifty miles later, I arrived in Fremont, just a few minutes after Nancy, shortly before noon. Fremont was founded in 1858 and named for John Charles Fremont, who led an expedition through the Platte valley in 1842. He also had figured prominently in California's history, playing a major role in the Bear Flag Revolt, the revolution that separated California from Mexico. We had lunch and wandered the downtown, shopping in a half dozen antique stores

I climbed up my first hill in some time as I left town, leaving the Platte River valley behind. We had been losing many of our traveling companions the last few days. The Pony Express, the Oregon Trail and California Trail all headed south toward Kansas City at Kearney. I-80 struck out for Lincoln and Omaha east of Grand Island, just as we turned north. The Interstate would continue across Iowa about 50 miles south of us. In Fremont, we left the Platte River and the Mormon Trail as they headed southeast to Omaha. The Union Pacific was still with us and the wail of the diesel locomotive's horn could still be heard at every crossing.

The road east to Blair, Nebraska, and the Missouri River was a twenty mile roller coaster ride of slow climbs and fast downhills and was a preview for what lay ahead in Iowa. The farms, with their freshly painted buildings, manicured lawns, and healthy fields reminded me of my home state as well. I saw two women out mowing their lawns, one with a hand mower and the other riding on a small green John Deere. After about the sixth hill, I imagined I would see the grain elevator in Blair, with the Missouri River flowing just beyond, but it was twelve or more hills before I finally rolled into town.

I found Nancy on Main Street in front of a video rental store and stopped for a drink before attempting to cross the river. I wasn't sure whether I could ride on the bridge, so Nancy waited and followed behind, in case I needed a ride. I stopped to take a picture of the highway and railroad bridges that ran parallel to each other across the river. A pickup zoomed by and a young guy leaned out of the window and yelled, "Get a car, asshole!" So after 1,800 miles of courtesy, I found intolerance right across the river from Iowa, the state where I spent the

Old post card view of the Missouri River bridge between Nebraska and Iowa.

first twenty-three years of my life. I was born in Garner, Iowa – population 2,000 – and grew up working in my father's two-cash-register grocery store, earned my Boy Scout cycling merit badge at fifteen, and attended a high school with less than 200 students.

"Cross the wide Missouri." It was a major milestone for me. I stopped halfway across the looked down at the "mighty Mo." It didn't seem that wide, but it was muddy and swift flowing and would have been a challenge for Lewis and Clark as they paddled north on their great voyage of discovery.

I rode into Iowa and finally completed my longest day so far – just under ninety miles. The day had been warm and climbing those hills was sweaty work. I felt about as fragrant as the cattle trucks that had passed me on my way into Fremont.

All the way to Lincoln Way.
All the way to Lincoln Way.

—Iowa State football cheer

CHAPTER SIX
Iowa

July 2 - Day 34
Missouri Valley to Westside
75.0 miles

I rode into town for breakfast under an overcast sky, serenaded by some early morning thunder. Nancy left for a hair appointment in Ames, a hundred and fifty miles away. We planned to meet in the afternoon. I had plotted a course that would take me off Highway 30 onto some less traveled roads. Highway 30 has a gravel shoulder and I was forced to either ride on the gravel or on a highway that was filled to overflowing with large vehicles traveling at high rates of speed. It hadn't been any fun the day before, on my way into town, after crossing the Missouri River. I had been warned to expect hills and hot weather by two of my Iowa buddies. So far, they were batting five hundred. It wasn't hot, but there were plenty of hills to climb, one nearly every mile. The Loess Hills of Iowa are impressive, with relatively short but steep ascents. The Union Pacific and the Lincoln Highway both headed northeast to avoid as many of these big bumps in southwest Iowa as they could. The downhills seemed brief, primarily because there was a wind out of the east. I appeared to be climbing a series of stairs out of the valley of the Missouri

As I climbed hill after hill, it was evident that the pace of the last several days was beginning to wear me down. By the end of the day, I would have biked for ten consecutive days, averaging sixty-six miles per day. In the last four days alone, I had ridden over three hundred miles. I was ready for a day off. My muscles were no longer as sore as they had been during my journey across Nevada, but cramps in the night were not uncommon. I felt good at the end of the day, but had lost much of my enthusiasm in the saddle. At least Iowa was green – the corn, the trees, the grass, even the weeds.

I stopped in Portsmouth and decided to rest and have a soft drink after two hours of hills and wind. I was directed to a restaurant near the road that led north out of town. I slowly drank my Coke in the bar at the 191 Club. I finished and started out the door. A delivery man took one look at me, hesitated, and then asked, "Which way you heading?" "North," I answered, "for about fifteen miles, and then east." He hesitated again and then said, "You really should go back in the bar and take a look at the television. There's a major storm just north

Facing page: An Iowa farm scene between Ames and Nevada.

of here. You could be riding right into it."

I returned to the bar and noticed that everyone was indeed watching the television which displayed Doppler radar of the surrounding area. In California, weather radar indicates the intensity of the rain by color – light or dark green for normal rain and, only occasionally, yellow for heavy rain. Well, thirty miles north of us in Denison, radar showed a dab of green, a bit of yellow and a large disturbing patch of red with a purple center, two entirely new levels of rainfall that I'd never seen on television in California. The purple center was the most violent and evidently had the potential to turn into a tornado. Here in Portsmouth people were moving their cars into garages and preparing for the worst. Riding a bike north towards Denison, as I had originally intended, didn't seem very wise right at that time. I decided to order another Coke and stick around the 191 Club for awhile and see which way this storm was moving. When they issued a tornado watch for the Portsmouth area, I decided to ask Brenda for a menu and ordered an excellent prime rib sandwich for lunch. I watched some tennis from Wimbledon and talked with many friendly people, while spending two hours waiting for the tornado watch to be lifted.

Above: A cross marks the spot where lightning proved fatal. Right: Darkening skies signal the arrival of an afternoon storm.

The sky still looked dark and rainy as I started north. Between five and ten inches of rain had fallen in the last two hours in the Denison area. I had stopped to put on my raincoat when a guy pulled up next to me and said, "Are you going north? It sure looks wet up there. Why don't you just stick around for the baseball game to-night?" I had waited long enough and decided to take my chances. Things worked out well for a while. I was going north and the wind was blowing out of the south. I was following a river valley, with only a few hills, and was making good time. I turned east for five miles and had difficulty with both wind and hills, but then turned north again. The south wind increased another notch or two and I took off like a rocket for nine swift miles.

I was on my way to Manilla to see Charlie and Loretta Schram, mom and dad of my good friend Ed Schram. After my rocket ride north, Manilla was only seven miles to the east. It took me over an hour to get

there. It was simply the most difficult experience I'd ever had on a bike. I was riding along an exposed ridge line, moving up and down, but constantly fighting the wind that was roaring in from the south. I reeled as a torrent of air slamming into me with a violence I'd never experienced, at least not on a bike. The wind would gust, bending the corn in the fields to the ground, picking me up and moving me three or four feet toward the center line of the road. I felt adrift in a green sea of corn stalks without an anchor, all other noises obscured by the harsh sweep of the wind. The violent storm that passed through north of here must have created these winds. I could hardly keep the bike upright and had to lean into the wind to maintain my balance. I would have stopped, but I wanted to see the Schrams and, more importantly, I was a long way from anywhere and my cell phone indicated "no service." Quitting was not an option.

I finally arrived, and soon found Charlie walking across Main Street, planning festivities for the next two days of the Fourth of July weekend. There was a bike rodeo, a bucket brigade, a parade and fireworks planned. I heard all about it while I consumed a chocolate shake and a large lemonade, courtesy of Loretta. Charlie had recently sold the building on Main Street where he had operated a grocery store for many years. He was excited about the big real estate deal that brought him the amazing windfall of one dollar. His building, which had been closed for many years, needed a lot of work. He was happy to get rid of the property and avoid paying any more taxes on it. Ed had also worked in his dad's grocery stores.

Since I was still unable to contact Nancy on my phone, I set off with the wind, heading north towards Highway 30. I crossed an angry creek, filled to overflowing with milk chocolate colored water, carrying the runoff from this afternoon's storm along with several tons of Iowa topsoil. About ten miles later, my phone rang. It was Nancy and we decided to meet in Westside, about twelve miles short of Carroll, my original destination. Seventy-five miles of wind and hills were plenty for this day.

Nancy looked stylish after her visit to the beauty parlor in Ames. We purchased some groceries in town and drove two miles south to Swan Lake State Park. About a hundred recreational vehicles were parked in the camp, preparing for the big Fourth of July weekend.

There was an amazing amount of energy and excitement in the camp despite the mud that was left over from the heavy rains. Kids, dogs, bikes and friendly people were everywhere. Adding to the festive air were flags flying in the stiff breeze and awnings decorated with strings of lights.

Our neighbors even lost their six year old son for two hours in the confusion. He disappeared on his bike, creating a flood of concern that flowed out in all directions from his parents' campsite, then reappeared as darkness fell. Campfires and wood smoke were the order of the day, or more accurately, the night. Since most

Busy campsite at Swan Lake State Park.

of the wood was wet, there was a lot of smoke, with sparks drifting into the dark sky. The fires were built in metal containers made out of old wheel rims, and lawn chairs surrounded the fires where hot dogs and marshmallows were roasted. It was still hot and humid at ten thirty and we continued to hope in vain for cooler weather. My hair was still wet from a shower I had taken over three hours ago.

July 3 - Day 35
Westside to Boone
70.6 miles

The camp at Swan Lake was relatively quiet when we pulled out after a pancake breakfast at 8:30. We drove back to Westside where I planned to ride into Carroll on a graveled piece of the Lincoln Highway. Although it lacked the hurricane force I'd run into the day before, there was still a hard wind blowing out of the south. It pushed the motor home around, rocking it from side to side, on our drive west.

On my bike, the combination of wind and gravel made me nervous. Coasting on my first downhill, I gripped the handlebars tightly, leaning into the wind. I worried that my tires would slip on the loose gravel at this faster speed, sending me sliding across the rough

Flag flies in a stiff breeze in a farm yard near Jefferson.

surface to disaster. I gradually gained confidence, but was working hard. It would take me forever to reach Carroll at this rate. After three miles, a sign informed me that the road was closed to through traffic, so I turned north and the gravel was history.

This put me back on Highway 30, the road I was trying to avoid by taking the gravel. Fortunately, the highway in this area was recently renovated, creating a paved shoulder nearly two feet wide. The wind moved around a bit to the west and gave me a little help. Suddenly, Highway 30 didn't look so bad. In one mile I crossed the Iowa State Divide – an experience not quite as exciting as crossing the Continental Divide in Wyoming. All the area to the west drained to the Missouri River and everything to the east to the Mississippi.

I stopped at a Casey's General Store in Carroll for a cold drink and discovered I had left my cell phone with Nancy in the motor home. I wouldn't be able to contact her. The road east out of Carroll had only a wide gravel shoulder and heavy traffic. I managed to stay on the pavement for short periods but was forced onto the gravel frequently by streams of cars. As I struggled along the rough shoulder, I decided it wasn't any worse than the gravel road I had survived earlier in the morning. It was a difficult fifteen miles, but finally I was able to turn off onto an old section of the Lincoln Highway. It paralleled Highway 30, about two miles to the south. Morning sunshine had given way to overcast. The sky in the southwest once again began to grow dark and ominous – gray streaks slanting out of the clouds – another sign that more rain was on the way.

The wind picked up and the new storm began chasing me with thunder rumbling overhead. It was still hot and humid and I was hungry and tired and wanted this day to end. I convinced my body that another ten miles of effort was acceptable, if lunch was waiting at the end.

In Jefferson, I found a pizza place on the square across from the courthouse. There was a statue of Abraham Lincoln in front of the building. A bronze, life-size Abe, standing on platform, eight feet high, looked down on the old highway that had been named after him. I talked the waitress into allowing me to use the phone to make a collect call to my friend Chuck Kolbe in Des Moines. Chuck then called Nancy and told her to meet me in Boone at Mamie Eisenhower's birthplace that afternoon.

After lunch, I had a delightful ride to Grand Junction. The sun was out and there were several old gas stations and motels that looked like they were built in the twenties. After Grand Junction, there was another long ride back on Highway 30. I was feeling exhausted again by the time I arrived in Ogden, another town with many Lincoln Highway banners. I went into a restaurant/bar and had two large ice teas and a Snickers to fuel me for the last eight miles into Boone. The two guys at the bar encouraged me. "You'll have a pretty ride to Boone, four miles down and four miles up."

It was indeed beautiful. Here in central Iowa, the descent to the Des Moines River was one of the most difficult sections of the Lincoln Highway and had caused many fatal accidents, especially in the winter. It wasn't the equal of the big hills out west, but I loved it. It was about a mile down and a mile up and the rest was fairly level. After seventy-two more miles and the eleventh straight day of riding, I was as ready for a break as I ever would be. Both Nancy and the motor home looked good when I arrived in Boone, and we wasted little time loading up and starting south to Des Moines.

After a short reunion with our friends Chuck and Sue Kolbe and a quick shower, we went out for dinner, and were joined by three other couples: a fraternity brother, his wife and four of their friends from Des Moines. The food was good and my aches and pains

Above right: A cut stone Lincoln Highway marker near Boone.
Above left: A notorious descent toward the Des Moines River
on the old Lincoln Highway east of Grand Junction.
Below: The birthplace of Mamie Eisenhower in Boone.

12,000 bicyclists test their mettle on the rolling hills of Iowa during the 1998 RAGBRAI (Register's Annual Great Bike Ride Across Iowa).

diminished as the evening continued. We checked into a hotel for the night, watched fireworks out the window and were soon asleep.

July 4 - Day 36
Des Moines
Rest Day

We joined Chuck and Sue the next morning in their condo, which was on the twelfth floor of a high-rise building across the street from our hotel. Chuck and I had joined the same fraternity, Tau Kappa Epsilon, at Iowa State during the fall of 1960, later rooming together and becoming good friends. Chuck and Sue married while in college and stayed in Iowa, while I moved to California. Time and distance reduced our friendship to Christmas cards and an occasional tele-

phone call until our daughter Whitney decided to attend Iowa State in 1994.

We began to see each other on a regular basis as Nancy and I began visiting Iowa twice a year. Soon Chuck convinced me that I should try to ride in RAGBRAI (Register's Annual Great Bike Ride Across Iowa). It's a week long ride across the state for ten or twelve thousand people sponsored by the *Des Moines Register,* and is about the most fun you can have on a bike. I trained hard in the spring and summer of 1996, hoping I would be ready to complete the ride and enjoy the party that flows along through the many small towns of Iowa. Chuck and I rode all 450 miles together and dipped the front wheels of our bikes into the Mississippi River in triumph. More than any other single event, this ride across Iowa, where I averaged nearly 65 miles a day, convinced me that I could ride across the country. A year later, while Chuck and Sue were on a training ride for RAGBRAI 1997, Chuck was struck by a car and was rushed to a hospital by helicopter. A spinal injury has him currently confined to a wheelchair.

Our Fourth of July celebration with the Kolbes began with a visit to Jimmy's restaurant for breakfast. It was after ten when our food arrived and I was famished. We returned to their home and watched the Wimbledon final. Chuck and his partners are cattle brokers, with an office in Red Oak, Iowa, where they sell "branded beef" and other meat products.

Chuck and I called our friend, Ed Schram, who lives in Santa Barbara. Ed, Chuck and I have remained good friends since we first met at Iowa State. We talked for over an hour and learned that Ed was building an elaborate tree house in his backyard. Later, we were joined by a reporter from the *Des Moines Register* who had heard about my cross-country ride and my connections with Iowa and Chuck. He asked some questions, took some notes and had us pose for a picture.

Chuck and Sue prepared a dinner that featured some delicious Iowa beef. We thanked them for their hospitality and vowed to get together again soon. It had been a perfect day for us to relax, rest, and heal a bit before we once again started on the trail. We drove back to Boone and checked into a motel. About 9:30 we heard a loud explosion, announcing the beginning of the fire works show. Outside we found a few dozen people sitting on the grass in front of the motel, in position to watch the display. We pulled our own lawn chairs out of the motor home, joined them and ended our Fourth perfectly, under a sky filled with the rockets' red glare.

July 5 - Day 37
Boone to Marshalltown
61.6 miles

I rode the Lincoln Highway to Ames over five miles of gravel without any significant problems. Riding into Ames was like entering a time warp, returning to my college days. The old football field, where I had spent many Saturday afternoons cheering the Iowa State Cyclones on to defeat, was at the southwest corner of the campus. They rarely won, but we continued to cheer, "All the way to Lincoln Way. All the way to Lincoln Way." This yell was used when the home team was headed south towards the main street, named Lincoln Way in honor of the Lincoln Highway. The men's gym, where my freshman basketball team practiced in 1960, was adjacent to the field. Lynn Avenue led off Lincoln Way to the Kappa House where my daughter Whitney had lived while attending Iowa State, as had my sister Barb earlier. Ash Avenue led to the TKE house where Chuck, Ed, my cousin Tom, and I had spent our days and nights.

So, I had completed the link – all the way to Lincoln Way – using my bike to connect Davis, California to Ames, Iowa, both on the Lincoln Highway. But I wasn't done. I still needed to conclude the ride – all the way to New York City on the island of Manhattan. If it hadn't been so hot, I might have even thought it possible.

Nancy called and said that Chuck and I had made the front page of the metro section of the *Des Moines Register*. I found a copy of the paper when I stopped for breakfast and gave Chuck a call while I waited for my omelette. The writer had done a reasonable job of describing the relationship between Chuck and me. There was even a picture of each of us, but we both felt that he had left out some of the good stuff. Whitney had been in the metro section of the Register the day she moved into the dorm, her first day at Iowa State back in 1994. They were interested in why a California girl would decide to come to Iowa to go to school. So we were keeping the Roe tradition alive.

Six women were sitting across from my booth and one of them leaned over towards me and asked, "Excuse me, you wouldn't be riding a bike, would you?" Dressed the way I was, it had to be obvious, but I de-

Beardshear Hall on the Iowa State University campus at Ames, then and now.

Signs from the top: A Lincoln Highway monument, the Niland Cafe in Colo and Shady Oaks in Marshalltown. Above right: Old houses along the road.

cided to play it straight. "I sure am." "Are you that guy that was in the Register today?" "Yeah, did you see that?" "You certainly have ridden a long ways." "It's nice to be in Iowa," I replied. My five minutes of fame for the day.

On the east side of Nevada, the town, not the state, there was a beautiful Lincoln Highway monument with a Lincoln quote. *"I believe that a man should be proud of the city in which he lives and that he should so live that his city will be proud that he lives in it."* I liked it.

Just east of Colo was the Niland Cafe, gas station and motor court, located at the junction of the Lincoln and Jefferson Highways. The Jefferson was another early named highway that extended from New Orleans to Winnipeg, Canada. The gas station was missing the gas pumps, but looked much like it must have looked sev-

enty years ago when it serviced that important intersection. Nancy met me for lunch in State Center, just after I repaired my fifth flat tire of the trip.

A month ago, I asked Mike Thieroff, my Highway 50 companion and cross-country veteran, if the days got a little easier after a couple weeks of riding. He thought for a moment and said, "No, it's pretty much a challenge each and every day." I thought he must be wrong or hadn't understood the question. Surely, it would have to get easier after riding four or five hours a day for several weeks. As I rode into Marshalltown, after another sixty mile day, I thought of Mike. He had been right. It wasn't getting a whole lot easier. It was hot – and humid – and I felt like I was baking inside my own skin. With the high humidity, perspiration doesn't pro-

Left: A old gas station recycled as a crafts shop in Montour.
Right: Shady Oaks in Marshalltown, the oldest campground west of the Mississippi River.

vide the same amount of cooling as it had in the drier western climate. If it was going to get easier, I wish it would start soon.

We camped at Shady Oaks, just east of Marshalltown, another major Lincoln Highway landmark. A huge grove of 150 year old oaks shaded the camp ground that had been a place of rest for travelers on the highway since 1926. It was easily one of the most beautiful places we had stayed. A few of the original buildings remained, including one of the eighteen cabins, a "dayroom" building where I took a long shower, and the office/home of the manager. There was also another, newer landmark at the campground. The owners began building a tree house in 1983, and have added a level, a point of interest or feature, every year. We toured

the tree house, guided by Judy Gift. The structure had eleven levels, reaching a height of fifty-five feet. The tree house had over five thousand square feet of deck and featured a television, several telephones, a microwave and a refrigerator. There were wonderful places to sit and enjoy the view of the meadow to the east, or to relax among the branches, looking out through the leaves, five stories above the ground.

Later, we walked around under the oaks in the growing darkness. Lightning bugs were everywhere, hundreds of them, floating up into the trees and gliding along the ground. Nancy called them stars in the grass. It was a perfect description for a miniature Milky Way.

July 6 - Day 38
Marshalltown to Cedar Rapids
73.3 miles

We were entertained with another whopper of storm during the night. The thunder was so loud that Nancy gave up trying to sleep, turned on her light and read for awhile. We both spent a restless night. Mary came over to see us in the morning, her cell phone held to her ear. She was trying to convince the local paper that they needed to come out and interview the Lincoln Highway cyclist. I was leaving in less than half an hour, so they declined. Mary, however, took some pictures and was going to attempt to place a story in my absence.

The day was fine as I left Shady Oaks and started out in search of breakfast. About an hour into the ride, I had another flat tire. Nancy's cell phone was not working in this service area, so I was unable to contact her. I used my single spare tube to fix the flat and set off down the road with a bad feeling. Another flat and I would be in trouble – no spare and no angel of mercy to come to the rescue. Since I was averaging less than one flat per week, I had at least one reason to be optimistic.

Suddenly, my phone rang. It was Channel 8, a Des Moines television station, and they had read the piece in the *Register* and wanted to do a story on the ride and my friendship with Chuck. I said fine, but I was 75 miles away from them. They checked with their news director and called back saying that the distance was too great. Another failed opportunity for stardom.

The most famous bridge in Tama has concrete railings that spell out LINCOLN HIGHWAY, one on either side of the road. It is a national landmark and a mecca for Lincoln Highway buffs. I guess perhaps I was becoming one. Just down the street is the Tower King Cafe that opened in 1925 to serve the highway. At one time there also was a gas station with a garage topped by a tower. Today only the restaurant survives. Finally, food. There was a wonderful sign in front that featured the head of an Indian chief. The town of Tama was famous in Iowa when I was growing up because it was the home of the Sauk and Fox Indian tribe.

Five or six miles beyond Tama, the dreaded disaster struck. Another flat. Now what? I stood next to my

bike, helplessly searching the cornfields for an answer, trying to think of a way around my problem. I didn't know what to do, so I walked a block or so back down the road to a farmhouse with a nice shady front yard. Still not sure what my plan of attack was going to be, I knocked on the back door. When no one answered, I opened the screen door, stuck my head in and shouted,

The Tama Bridge, a famous Lincoln Highway landmark.

"Anybody home?" a few times. Evidently not. I walked into the kitchen and shouted again. No answer. That's far enough, I thought, so I turned around and retreated out the door. I thought about trying to repair one of my tubes, but didn't feel confident that a repaired tube would last me for another fifty miles when two new tubes had failed during the last twenty-five.

I returned to the front yard and decided to call an Iowa State architecture classmate who lived up the road in Cedar Rapids. Don's son, Jay Primus, was at home when I called and he agreed to run three new tubes out to me, a distance of over forty miles each way. I was

saved, or I would be saved in an hour or so. As soon as I finished talking to Jay, Mrs. Ferguson pulled up in a sport utility vehicle. She was going over to look in her mail box, when she noticed me walking towards her, out of her front yard. I have to give her credit, she neither ran nor screamed and seemed quite calm as I explained my problem to her. While I waited for my new tubes, she brought me a large glass of ice water and encouraged me to rest on her front porch, where there was a comfortable chair in the shade.

As I lay stretched out in the shade on the floor of the porch, my shoes off and my feet propped up, I thought, "Well, for a disaster, this is actually pretty pleasant." Potted geraniums hung in a row from the ceiling, three flags flapped in the breeze, and a pile of kittens lay curled together next to the front door. From the corner of the porch, a pair of swallows were flying in and out of a nest with tidbits for their young. The view to the west, across the fields and down to the forest land that ran along the Iowa river, was fabulous. I was nearly asleep when Jim Ferguson drove into the driveway. I grabbed my shoes and walked over to explain my situation to him, but it turned out that he already knew who I was. He had read the article in the *Register* the day before and had many questions about the trip.

A post card of the King Tower Cafe, another Lincoln Highway landmark just down the road.

Jim was a livestock feed salesman and had even sold feed in Garner, my home town. He was concerned about the economy in rural Iowa. "It takes over two dollars to produce a bushel of corn and the price today is a buck eighty. Soy beans cost five dollars a bushel to produce and the price is less than four dollars. Same with hogs; it costs more than forty cents a pound to produce the pork and the price is only twenty-eight cents. People who have worked all their lives, people in their fifties, are losing equity each and every year. I don't know what they are going to do. Many of them feel that they are too

Top: A collection of metal advertising signs and an ancient tractor at an old gas station in Belle Plain. Below: A neon sign announces the Lincoln Cafe in Belle Plain.

old to find another job, but if they keep farming, they will have nothing left for retirement."

Jay arrived with my tubes and I thanked him. I wanted to give him a hug. He claimed he was glad to be of help and definitely was interested in the trip. He wanted to know what roads I had taken across the west. We all talked, I repaired my flat and, all too soon, I shook hands with two splendid people and started down the road. Twelve miles later, I arrived in Belle Plain, an old railroad town that was a highway archeologist's dream. Little has changed from the twenties when this was a major stop on the old highway. There was an old gas station, the building covered with dozens of automobile-related signs, the office filled with Lincoln Highway memorabilia. The owner – who recently passed away – of this rather amazing attraction was on the Johnny Carson show several years ago. A block down the road is the Lincoln Cafe where I had lunch. The double track of the transcontinental railroad continued through the cornfields next to the highway. It seemed like a long time since we followed it up over the Sierra Nevada mountains in California.

I was running way behind schedule and wondered how I might contact Nancy when my phone rang. Her phone had started working again when she arrived in Cedar Rapids and, since it was after 3:30, she called to see where I was. I had completed forty-three miles, but I still had thirty miles to go. She went to do errands and I continued to pump up hill after hill as the afternoon slipped away.

We met up at 6:30 and drove out to a state park camp site east of town. It was a beautiful afternoon now that I was off the bike. We called the Primus family and invited them out for breakfast. Then we called our son Eric and made arrangements to meet him in Pittsburgh. He was joining us for a week to ride with me across Pennsylvania. The long hot day was followed by a beautiful, cool night.

July 7 - Day 39
Cedar Rapids to Clinton
85.9 miles

We joined Marcia and Don Primus for breakfast in Cedar Rapids. Don and I have followed similar paths after receiving our degrees in architecture from Iowa State. His company designs, builds and manages commercial and office properties in this part of Iowa, while my company does the same thing with apartments back in Davis. It was great to dine with friends and share family stories.

After breakfast, I didn't feel good and wasn't looking forward to the ride. We drove back to the center of Cedar Rapids where I had stopped the day before. I had over eighty miles to go and I was getting a late start. I pulled on my bike clothes, slathered on the sun block, unloaded the bike off the back, filled the CamelBak with water, cleaned my sun glasses and checked to see what I might have forgotten – telephone, money, film, maps. It was all there. The routine almost seemed painful. I had successfully avoided boredom on the road to this point, but the exotic newness of the journey had worn off and the physical challenge of the mountains were well behind me. I needed a strategy to deal with Iowa.

I rode away as Nancy was on her way to have the motor home refrigerator repaired. Nothing was working

Antique store display:
A Lincoln Highway cigar box
and a milk bottle from the
Lincoln Highway Dairy.

right: the refrigerator, Nancy's telephone, my flat tires. After a couple of miles I discovered that I didn't feel quite that bad. I drank a lot water and rode hard. Nine miles out of town there was another "seedling mile," the first paved section of the Lincoln Highway in Linn County, constructed in 1918. The roadway had a long crack on either side, where three feet of pavement had been added to give it a more contemporary width. I got off my bike, paced off the distance and found that the original highway was only about eighteen feet wide.

Fifteen miles from Cedar Rapids, I arrived in Mt. Vernon. Cornell College was on the west side of the town and had a number of wonderful old stone and brick buildings sitting amidst acres of grass and old trees. I decided that Iowa was the riding lawn mover capital of the nation. There were more large expanses of grass, both in town and out, than I have ever seen. Farms had huge lawns near the house and then planted and mowed the ditch next to the road for a quarter mile or so on either side of the house. I watched one family work in tandem, the guy driving a tractor that pulled a large, ten-foot wide mower while his wife drove a riding mower and did the detail work. Even in town an acre of lawn was not uncommon.

I stopped at an antique store in downtown Mt. Vernon to check their post card stock and met two delightful women who wanted to know everything about my journey. One even took my picture. I called Nancy and told her not to miss this place – it's the kind of town that should be used as a movie set. She reported that

A brick section of the original highway preserved in Mt. Vernon.

Ed and Pam at Ketelsen RV had pushed her to the head of the line and fixed the refrigerator. Two more really nice people. As I set off out of town, I discovered my blues had faded in the morning sunshine. I had met some nice people and was feeling good, but I still had sixty miles to go.

In the town of Stanwood at Ditto's Cafe I ordered the "Super Pork Tenderloin" with fries, a lettuce salad and the "Jumbo Milk Shake." The milk shake was a challenge just by itself. There were two additional portions held in reserve in the stainless steel container the waitress sat on my table. My appetite was fine; maybe it was just my breakfast that was bad. I watched the waitress fill a root beer mug with an inch and a half of boiling water and then stick a fork in the glass. I was curious to see what she was making, but she walked into the back of the cafe carrying the glass. When she returned, I asked her what she was making in root beer mug, filled with hot water, and a fork. She laughed and said, "The catsup bottle lids get really icky, so I give them a hot bath, stirring them clean with the fork. After a couple minutes, my lids are spick-and-span, just like new." Well, I thought, you can learn something every day.

In Clarence, I stopped to take a picture of an old gas station that had been converted into a snack shop, when a fellow rode by on his bike. He waved to me and, after continuing down the road for a block, turned around and came back toward me. I waited for him in the shade under a big tree. He asked me where I was going and I told him about my cross-country, Lincoln Highway trip. I met Ron Smith and asked him what he was doing. I discovered that I might not be the only eccentric person riding around on a bike under the hot Iowa sun. "Well, there are 1,163 towns in the state of Iowa," he said, "according to the official Iowa Department of Transportation map. Their maps are the best, with up to date, accurate information. I retired not too long ago and I've been riding my bike to every single town in Iowa. I still have about ninety towns to go. Today I'm picking up a few of the towns I've missed in this area." I was amazed and wondered how many miles he had ridden over the hills of Iowa.

He asked if I had ever ridden in RAGBRAI, the bike ride across Iowa. "Yeah, I rode it twice, once last year and once three years ago." He said he had ridden in it the last seven years. He and his wife had an unusual approach. "We leave our home in Cedar Rapids and ride west on our bikes to the start of the route on the Missouri River. Then we ride across the state as a participant in the event. It's about our favorite week in the year. After RAGBRAI is over, we ride back home to Cedar Rapids from the Mississippi River. It usually is about a 900 mile round trip." And to think that I had been proud when Chuck and I had ridden all of the 450 miles of RAGBRAI three years ago. I decided that Ron Smith should live in Davis with all the other "bike nuts."

However, there are levels of craziness in every field. Ron would not yet qualify as a world class bike nut. For instance, Danny Chew won the 1999 Race Across America (RAAM) in a time of 8 days, 7 hours, 34 minutes. Riding from Irvine, California to Savannah, Georgia, he crossed seven states, covered 2,936 miles and rode in temperatures that exceeded 100 degrees on the last five days of the event. His nearest competitor finished only one hour and seventeen minutes behind him. RAAM is called the world's longest and most grueling bicycle race. They would get no argument from me. Contestants attempt not to sleep at all, but find the race too long to avoid sleeping between one and three hours per day.

Iowa, where 4-H was started, had been more difficult than I anticipated because of my 4 Hs – heat, humidity, hills and head winds. There were also the thunderstorms, the potential tornados, the long distances, and the roads without paved shoulders. In Wheatland, I stopped and bought a drink at Dave's Super Valu food store. My dad and mom had owned and managed Roe's Super Valu in Garner for forty years and, as I told Dave in Wheatland, I had done it all – sacked and carried out groceries, stocked shelves, inventoried, cut meat, prepared produce, swept floors and completed the weekly bookkeeping. "My first job was sorting pop bottles for fifteen cents an hour." He seemed impressed – at least a little.

I caught up with a pair of riders wearing green tee-shirts. Let me rephrase that. I quickly caught up and passed two riders who had been far in front of me. OK, they weren't ready to compete in the Tour d'France, but I am usually the one that was being passed by other bike riders. This father and son team were on their way to Erie, Pennsylvania, where they live. They had just started their trip in Cedar Rapids and looked a little weary, especially the father. They were working on a multi-year cross country trip, about 10 or 12 days at a time. Last year, they rode from Cape Cod to Erie. This year was Cedar Rapids to Erie, but Highway 30 had made the first day difficult. Their maps weren't good enough to allow them to find those sections of the old road that I had enjoyed so much. The father said they had been

forced to ride on the gravel shoulder for at least forty-five miles after they left Cedar Rapids. I rose out of my saddle, waved good-by and sprinted away down the road, feeling good. Hi, ho, silver, away!

The last ten miles of this 85 mile day I wasn't doing any sprinting. I was tired. I was hanging on and wishing that the town of Clinton was not so far away. The road became broken and patched in the city, difficult to ride on, and the traffic was heavy. I had estimated that I was going to travel no more than eighty miles on my way to Clinton. Each mile after eighty seemed to take forever. I received a call from Mary at Shady Oaks campground in Marshalltown. She told me that we had made the local paper and she wanted to send us a copy. It was seven in the evening before I found the camp, took off my shoes and drank a bottle of Arizona iced tea, without once taking it away from my lips, all twenty fluid ounces. Tomorrow we would cross the Mississippi. The mighty river was only a few hundred yards east of our camp and signified to me that less than a third of the trip remained.

An original section of the narrow old Lincoln Highway near Stanwood.

*It is by riding a bicycle that you learn the contours of a country best,
since you have to sweat up the hills and coast down them.
. . . you have no such accurate remembrance of country you have driven through
as you gain by riding a bicycle.*

—Ernest Hemingway

CHAPTER SEVEN

Illinois

July 8 - Day 40
Clinton to Rochelle, IL
72.0 miles

As I approached the bridge spanning the Mississippi, I again worried that I might not be able to ride across. But, I found a walkway on the north side. This was a significant milestone, the river of Tom Sawyer and Huck Finn, the "Father of Waters," and "Old Man River" who just keeps rolling along. Other lyrics from that song also came to mind: ". . . *we sweat and strain, body all achin' and racked with pain,*" and "*I get weary and sick of trying.*" Sounds a lot like bike riding, especially in the afternoon.

In Fulton I turned back through town and rode out to a path that ran along the levee next to the river. I found a couple who were out for a walk and asked them to take my picture with the river and bridge behind me. I still had the Ohio, the Delaware, the Hudson and a several other rivers to cross, but at least another state was behind me. In Dixon, there was a sign that announced that Ronald Regan had been born there. Previous towns had claimed to be the home to high school state individual wrestling champions. The towns seemed equally proud of their native sons and had produced

signs that were about the same size.

The National Headquarters of the Lincoln Highway Association was located in Franklin Grove, an important destination for us. I had called ahead to make sure the office would be open, but nobody answered the phone and I could only leave a message on an answering machine. I was prepared to be disappointed when I rode up to the building, but I found a note taped to the window from Lynn Asp, the office manager. It invited us into the building to look around and also gave us directions to a historic site south of town where Lynn and Jack Kelley were working.

On the outskirts of town we found a saltbox house, a school, a blacksmith shop and a few other buildings that had been moved from other parts of the region. They

The Dixon Arch over the Lincoln Highway.
Facing page: A nice day in Chicago on the Navy Pier with the famous skyline in the background.

Out in front, next to the building was a red and white billboard-sized sign with large blue lettering, LINCOLN HIGHWAY. Above that, in smaller red letters, it said, "New York 999" and "Frisco 2384" – underneath, "Clinton 53" and "Chicago 93." There on the sign was a summary of the day and our trip. The sign was beautiful to me, especially the numbers. We posed for pictures before shaking hands and saying goodbye to Jack and Lynn.

Rochelle was another seventeen miles down the road. Since there was no camp in the area, Nancy went ahead to find a motel, while I completed my seventy-two mile day. She found a small motel that looked perfect initially, and we checked in. I even took a shower. But we quickly discovered that our neighbors were not the kind of people you'd want to invite home to meet your mother. I walked past the open door of one of units. A bearded man with sunken eyes sat on the edge of the bed looking out at me, a sack clutched in his lap. I waved and said hello. He responded with a growl. Gangsters have used motels as hideouts. Bonnie & Clyde fought it out at the Red Crown Motel in Missouri, dying after they left another motel in a hail of bullets in 1934. John Dillinger holed up in a roadside camps. One of his favorites was the Little Bohemia Cabins in Spider Lake, Wisconsin.

We moved to the motor home – the room smelled of smoke – eating some cheese and crackers and looking at each other, trying to decide if we really wanted to endure a night in this place. We finally just returned the key, abandoned the $35 we had paid for the place and drove down the road a mile. We checked into a wonderful new AmeriHost Inn for $55, a decision we never regretted.

Top: Lincoln Highway headquarters in Franklin Grove. Above: A sign in Rochelle.

were all in various stages of renovation. We also found two enthusiastic people who toured us through their projects and then persuaded me to try a spear thrower. They were evidently the rage a few centuries ago. The thrower is a slotted stick that will hold a spear and give leverage and power to your throw. It worked pretty well. I managed to hit a large hay bale, about half the time, from a distance of fifty feet.

Back in town we were shown the work that had been completed on the H. I. Lincoln Building, an old stone structure that was the office and headquarters for the Lincoln Highway Association. A relative of Abe had constructed the building in the middle of the nineteenth century. Jack pointed out what was original and what was new. It was difficult to differentiate between the two without his help, and this was in a building that had been totally gutted when they started. "We were able to see outlines on the walls where cabinets had been located. These outlines showed us the size and shape of the cabinetwork and even the type of mouldings that were used. We found that the stone walls were out of plumb so we had to winch the upper part of the south wall over six inches and then re-chink the joints."

July 9 - Day 41
Rochelle to Aurora
50.9 miles

It was raining steadily in the morning after a stormy night. Since we were enjoying a comfortable motel that offered a complementary breakfast, we were in no hurry to leave. The weather remained overcast and cool, but the rain stopped. About nine-thirty, I was headed for DeKalb. Let's see, cool, overcast, a nice tail wind, a road with a three-foot paved shoulder, and a relatively short, fifty mile trip planned. This could be an easy day. Two miles later I lost the paved shoulder and traffic increased dramatically. Trucks were streaming past, sending me off onto the gravel. I revised my prediction.

DeKalb is the home of the University of Northern Illinois. I liked the appearance of the downtown and thought seriously about stopping for lunch, but pushed on. I still had half an hour of riding remaining until noon. Forty-five minutes later, I found Earl's Corner in Maple Grove, my last chance for food until Geneva twenty miles away. I walked in and was the only customer in the place. A young, short, significantly overweight woman was behind the bar. I asked her if she was serving lunch. She didn't say a word, just handed me a menu. After I ordered a hamburger, she returned to the kitchen to cook it. So she was bartender, waitress and cook. Small staff. Chicago Bears football posters and Bulls basketball posters covered the walls and ten tables were all set with napkins, placemats and silverware in the dining room.

My hamburger and fries returned from the kitchen, but the woman had little to say. I thought maybe she didn't like my looks, but I asked her about the posters anyway. "I really don't pay much attention to sports. My dad is a big fan." I tried again and asked her about an alternate route that would take me off the busy highway.

She came over and looked at my map and recommended a road just two miles to the south. We began to talk about my trip and her life in Maple Grove. Her husband had just won the lottery, a prize of $16,000. The two of them were in the middle of an amicable divorce. "He gave me almost half the winnings and we are still friends after splitting everything. We have a four year old son, so I wanted him to have a father and not a lot of bad feelings." I congratulated her on the way they had worked things out.

The road to Geneva proved to be smooth and fast, the wind propelling me along the road at over twenty miles per hour. Geneva is on the Fox River and deserved more time than the half-hour I could spend. Then Nancy called and said she was waiting in Aurora near a river boat gambling complex. She had also found a store with a replacement hubcap for the one we lost off the motor home in Nevada.

I found a bike path along the river, where I traveled in shade and solitude. The trees formed a cool green canopy and the river came into view occasionally on my left. Residences and lawns showed up irregularly on my right, then nothing but the forest and the quiet. I arrived in Aurora and found Nancy waiting next to the bike path. It had been easy day.

After loading up we started to Hinsdale and a two-day rest with my sister and brother-in-law, Barbara and Dick Kasperek. The traffic was heavy and a red light seemed to be blocking our way every few minutes. The twenty-five mile drive to their home took nearly an hour. That night, I retired to a bed that didn't require a ladder to get into and went to sleep in a room that wouldn't be driving along the highway the next day.

Two vintage theaters:
Geneva (above) and Aurora.

July 10 - Day 42
Hinsdale
Rest Day

The luxury of leisure – rising late, reading the paper, eating breakfast, talking with family, contemplating the morning, and deciding what activity, if any, to undertake first. Barb and Dick's daughter Morgan was playing in a basketball tournament with her high school team. Morgan at fifteen was already a veteran on the varsity team. The tournament had over fifty college coaches in the audience, many seated on the floor near the players with their clipboards in hand.

Morgan is a 6'1" post player, and already very good. We enjoyed watching as she and her teammates overpowered another team, nearly doubling their opponent's score. After the game we drove to Evanston for a quick look at Northwestern University and the beautiful houses near Lake Michigan. We returned to see another equally lopsided victory with Morgan flashing her offensive skills, and then to Hinsdale for lunch. I remain amazed at the amount of food I consume. It will be interesting to see what happens to my appetite when I hang my bike on the back of the motor home and start

Two scenes from the Navy Pier: Dick Kasperek and Nancy in photo at right.

driving back to California.

The afternoon was spent watching the U.S. women play China in World Cup soccer. The scoreless duel lasted ninety minutes of regular time and two fifteen minute overtimes and was finally decided when the U.S. won, five to four, in a penalty kick shoot-out. It had been an exciting, relaxing day, nearly devoid of physical activity.

July 11 - Day 43
Hinsdale
Rest Day

Two views of Chicago's magnificent architecture. Left: The Wrigley Building and Tribune Tower dominated the skyline for decades.

After coffee, the Sunday paper and french toast, Dick drove us into Chicago. We parked the car at the Navy Pier, the city's most popular destination, on a perfect summer day. The pier was crowded, Lake Michigan stretching across the horizon to the east and the skyline of the city soaring into the clouds in the west. There were dozens of restaurants, a twelve story ferris wheel, large sculptures lining the edge of the pier and live music drifting into the crowd every few hundred feet. We found the kiosk selling tickets for the architectural boat tour of the downtown and purchased three for the one o'clock voyage.

Chicago's reputation for good architecture is well deserved. Louis Sullivan tutored Frank Lloyd Wright here. The Wrigley Building, the Tribune Tower and the Merchandise Mart are three older buildings that dominated the Chicago skyline decades before the John Hancock and the Sears Tower, both in the 1,400 foot range, dwarfed them. We traveled up the Chicago River under the bridge carrying Michigan Avenue over the river, gazing up at Marina Towers and skyscrapers designed by famous architects from around the world. Walls of glass reflected the clouds and the facades of the buildings near them. An Amtrak train ran along the river under buildings built on air rights purchased from the railroad. I was fascinated by the warehouses being converted into lofts and the condominiums going up near the water. People were moving back into the center of the city. We returned to the pier for lunch in a sidewalk cafe, sat back and watched the passing parade.

Before returning to Hinsdale, we drove up Michigan Avenue past all the exclusive shops and an amazing collection of cows. The city of Chicago had commissioned three or four hundred artists to paint or decorate fiberglass, life-sized cows. They were placed all over the center of town, along the lake, in front of the opera house, on top of a bridge, and along the length of Michigan Avenue. The cows were drawing huge crowds downtown. They were wonderful, whimsical, colorful and entertaining. As we drove down the avenue, we found people posing for photographs next to their favorite cows. The cows will be sold at auction in the fall, raising money for a variety of charities. Nancy thought a similar project might work for Davis with pigs or frogs – pigs, because of our agricultural history and college; frogs because the mayor of Davis was featured on national television when she led the fight to build a $20,000 "toad tunnel" that has never been used.

July 12 - Day 44
Aurora to Deep River, Indiana
73.7 miles

I faced the challenge of trying to squeeze around Chicago and its suburbs and the eight million people who live there, avoiding as many of these people as possible. Since it was Monday and everyone was back at work, it would not be an easy task. I started down the bikepath, next to the river, and less than a block later hit a dead end. I wandered through the city, trying to follow bike path signs. After about a mile, I gave up on the path and started south on Lincoln Avenue. I soon found another bike route. The gravel trail meandered through a residential neighborhood, crossing a street every block or so. I felt like I was going in the right direction, but I couldn't fig-

ure out where I was on my map. I guess I was lost. Before long the path ended, I turned south and immediately found Highway 30. Not lost.

The road was terrible – poor surface, tons of traffic (much of it trucks) and no shoulder at all. Fortunately, I only needed it for a mile and I was able to exit onto a secondary road. Nancy called when I was just of few miles out of Plainfield to say she was pwarked on Main Street in front of an antique store with thousands of postcards. I asked her to check on a bike shop. My rear

wheel had been knocked out of line when we backed out of the driveway in Hinsdale a few hours earlier. Luck was with me – there was a bike shop four doors down. I arrived and found there were several bikes to be repaired before they could work on mine. When I told the employees in the shop about my trip and asked them if they could help me out, the mechanic agreed to drop what he was doing and work on my bike. I walked down the street to check out the post cards. Nancy, of course, had made friends with all the storekeepers and they had

Above: The Father of Highways, the Lincoln Highway, meets the Mother Road, Route 66, on Plainfield's Main Street. Right: Downtown Joliet with a bridge across the Des Plaines River.

lots of questions about the ride. I found a dozen interesting cards – several on the Lincoln Highway – and returned to find the bike waiting for me, ready to resume my journey.

The guy at the bike shop recommended I avoid the highway and go east to follow a frontage road along a freeway that would carry me most of the way to Joliet. He also warned me to be careful in Chicago Heights, an extension of the south side of Chicago. He thought it would be a dangerous place to be riding by myself.

The ride was short, noisy along the freeway, and uneventful. Joliet had some wonderful old buildings in the downtown and a series of old bridges that crossed the Des Plaines River. Joliet was where the Lincoln Highway crossed old Route 66, the meeting of the father of U.S. highways with the "Mother Road." Highway 66 was the road that ran, as the song says, from Chicago to L.A. and is the one historic highway that is undoubtedly more famous than the Lincoln. Route 66 ended at the Santa Monica pier on the Pacific Ocean.

I stopped to take a picture of an old theater and visit the restored Union Station. As I was leaving town, I noticed an inviting tavern on the other side of the road with a long row of flower boxes in front of the parking lot. Zobel's looked like the perfect place for lunch.

I walked in and discovered that Zobel's was a railroad tavern. Joliet has been a major rail junction for years. A model railroad ran around the room just below the ceiling, while posters and pictures of trains and a trophy buck decorated the walls. Six or seven guys sat at the bar drinking beer. The bartender was a tall, friendly, raw boned woman with a blond pony tail. She was wearing an over-sized T-shirt with "What Part of No Didn't You Understand?" emblazoned on the front. When I asked about food, she frowned, shook her head and said, "Well, we have frozen pizza and microwave sandwiches. The

The Rialto Theater in Joliet.

An inviting bike path follows an old railroad east of Joliet.

pizza's not that bad, but I'd skip the sandwiches." I was disappointed, thinking I'd have to leave this pleasant spot and move on to find some food. Then she opened a large freezer and said, "Oh, wait a minute. We also have some homemade flour tacos I can heat up. They're actually not that bad." I ordered two of the tacos and an RC cola. "Good choice," she said and then smiled. "I really don't think the sandwiches are all that tasty."

I began talking to the fellow next to me, a retired steel worker. I was, of course, dressed in my bike togs, lycra from knee to neck. At six foot four, I'm fairly conspicuous anyway, but wearing a tight, hot pepper cycling shirt, I am a sight to behold, especially walking into a Joliet, Illinois tavern in the middle of the day. Eventually the steel worker asked me what I was up to. Soon, everyone in the bar knew I was on a cross country bike trip. The bartender was astonished. "You know, I've read about people like you in the paper or seen stories on television, but I've never have a chance to meet any of them. Now, you just walk into my bar." The next thing I knew she had returned my four dollars for the tacos and the cola and said, "Lunch is on me. Anyone who rides that far deserves a free meal."

The guy on my left complained loudly, "Hey, I come in here all the time and I never get a free meal. I've never even had a free drink. I'm guess I'll go out and get me a ten-speed." His buddy sitting next to him worried, "You might have a problem unless that bike's reinforced. How much do you weigh?" It turned out that he weighed a shade over 280 pounds. Then everyone joined in. When did you start? How far have you gone? When will you get to New York? Do you have a job? How did you get all that time off? Are you by yourself? The questions rained down. It was fun. A man at the other end of the bar bought me a drink, a second RC cola. I went out to my bike and retrieved a copy of the newspaper clipping from Nebraska that Nancy had given me before I left in the morning. "You seemed interested; I thought you might enjoy these." The bartender took them, glanced through them and asked, "Would you autograph them for me?" I couldn't believe it. "Sure." I wrote, "To the crew at Zobel's, good food and the best company in Joliet. Best Wishes," and signed, "Bill Roe." Before I could leave, every single guy in the bar walked over to me to make sure he didn't miss out on a handshake with the celebrity. I felt like Michael Jordan. I walked out of Zobel's shaking my head, a grin on my face that stretched from ear to ear.

Not too far out of Joliet, I located a brand new sixteen mile bike path south of Highway 30, another piece of the puzzle that I had worked on to get safely from point A to point B on this particular day. The path followed an old railroad line. For much of the way, I rode through a nature sanctuary with trees arching over the path, and swampland appearing on one or both sides. Occasionally a farm or a subdivision would slide by. I had only a few fellow travelers: some people riding bikes, a few others on rollerblades, and some just out for a stroll. It was a welcome relief from the constant concerns of riding along a busy road, looking into my rear view mirror, hoping I wouldn't have to turn onto the gravel shoulder to avoid a truck.

Nancy was waiting for me near the Indiana border and we agreed to keep going east, closer to a camp that we found southwest of Valparaiso. Just outside of Dyer, Indiana, I found a monument to the "Ideal Section" of the Lincoln Highway. This section of the highway, constructed just before 1920, featured what was then the ultimate of road-building achievement – concrete paving on four traffic lanes, a roadside park and lighting provided by the General Electric Company.

I felt pretty good after a seventy-five mile ride. It

A monument to "The Ideal Section" of the Lincoln Highway.

had obviously helped to take two days off. Our camp proved to be a friendly place with visits from two former Californians, one from Sacramento and one who had lived in Laguna Beach.

*It is delightful to read on the spot
the impressions and opinions of tourists
who visited a hundred years ago,
in the vehicles and with the aesthetic prejudices
of the period, the places you are visiting now.
The voyage ceases to be a mere tour through space;
you travel through time and thought as well.*

—Aldous Huxley

CHAPTER EIGHT
Indiana

**July 13 - Day 47
Deep River to
Plymouth**
59.5 miles

What a difference a day makes. The day before I felt fine after a long ride. Now, I was tired after twenty miles and still had miles to go before I finished. The road seemed endless and my legs lifeless. I missed the first turn into Valparaiso and doubled back to visit the downtown, costing me four additional miles. The mistake bothered me more that it should have. I lectured myself, "You should have just kept going. You'd be five or ten miles closer to being off the bike and Valparaiso wasn't all that interesting anyway." I argued back, "If all you wanted to do was ride a bike and not see anything new, you might as well have stayed at home." Valparaiso was pretty nice, with a courthouse square and several blocks of well preserved older buildings. People were sitting outside of a bakery enjoying the sunshine, having coffee and pastries.

I ventured off Highway 30 to ride another piece of the Lincoln Highway. It was a mess, absolutely the worst stretch of road I had been on during the entire trip. My bike bounced and banged over the broken pieces of pavement for three miles. It felt like I was riding on a jackhammer. My hands and rear end were badly abused and I was soon arguing with myself again about the wisdom of leaving my smooth, boring road. West of Hamlet, a town that wasn't even as big as its name, the pavement improved. Here I found Waymire's Corner Tap and it was well past time for lunch. Inside, it was more restaurant than a bar, with blue and white checkered tablecloths brightening the room. A couple in their early sixties was finishing lunch at one of the tables, a man was sitting at the counter and a waitress was standing near the back of the dining room. She greeted me when I walked in.

My entrance again created a small stir, even after I removed my helmet and my wraparound sun glasses with the small rear view mirror attached. Inevitably, I was asked what I was doing. The couple, in this case,

*A whimsical Indiana mailbox.
Facing page: A rusty old sign
outside a lunch room in Inwood.*

seemed especially interested in my trip. During our discussion, I learned that their son had ridden from San Diego to Georgia in the early seventies. The man described how his son and a friend flew to the west coast and spent the afternoon putting together their new Schwin bikes. They had a free day before the start of their trip, so they rode out to the San Diego Zoo where both bikes were promptly stolen. The son wired home for funds to buy new bikes and they started over.

Suddenly the woman got up, came over to my table, sat down, introduced herself, pulled out a pencil and opened up a notebook. Ida Chipman was a free lance writer and photographer for two different local newspapers and wanted to do a story about my trip. The most difficult question was always, "Why are you doing this?" I mentioned a mid-life crisis, but the answer continued to be a work in progress. Perhaps, by the end of the ride, I'd know. We concluded the interview and went outside to take a picture in front of the restaurant.

Ida and her husband were leaving that weekend to go back to Annapolis. He graduated from the Naval Academy and was still involved with his alma mater. They left shortly before I did, wishing me a safe journey. I finished my lunch and went up to the counter to pay and the cashier told me, "The judge got it. It's all paid for." I learned that Ida's husband was a judge at the Center County Courthouse in Plymouth. That was two days in a row that I'd received a free lunch.

I hurried the last fifteen miles into Plymouth, and Nancy called just as I was turning onto the main street. She wanted me to visit the local museum because they had an interesting exhibit on the Lincoln Highway. I enjoyed the exhibit and the people at the little museum. We didn't stay long and were soon started north to South Bend, twenty-two miles away and the home of Leslie Whitcomb, great grandfather of Nancy Whitcombe Roe.

The Golden Dome at Notre Dame University in South Bend.

Nancy's dad added the "e" to their name after he moved away from home.

We stopped briefly at an antique store and learned that there were no Whitcombs listed in the phone book. An officer who worked for the sheriff's department knew that the old Whitcomb and Keller office building was on the corner of Jefferson and Lafayette in downtown South Bend. On the way we paid a visit to Notre Dame

Jesus," a mural on a high rise office building facing the stadium. Jesus is shown with his arms raised in the air, just like a referee signaling a touchdown.

We went downtown, looking for evidence that the office building on the southeast corner of Jefferson and Lafayette was indeed the former Whitcomb and Keller building. I stopped a man walking by and asked what he knew about the building. He turned out to be the Director of Historical Preservation for the city and county and, as one might imagine, was perhaps the most perfect person in all of Indiana that I could have stopped to ask this question. He invited us up to his office on the eleventh floor of the county building located just across the street, and gave us a half dozen books on historical neighborhoods in South Bend. Many of them had several homes built by Whitcomb and Keller. He also suggested we visit Riverview Cemetery and the main library's historical resource room. It was nearly seven in the evening and we were hungry and still had to find a place to stay. Our search for Nancy's roots would have to wait until tomorrow.

"Touchdown Jesus" near Notre Dame's football stadium.

July 14 - Day 46
Plymouth to Columbia City
42.4 miles

We drove over to Riverview Cemetery where we found acres of trees, tombstones, grass and mausoleums, but discovered that the office would be closed for another hour. We decided not to search for the needle in the haystack, but to return later to see if Leslie, or any other of the Whitcombs, were buried there.

Just east of downtown was a large subdivision developed by Whitcomb and Keller called Sunnymeade.

University. The central campus area in front of the Golden Dome was a park with a formal corridor of shrubs and flowers surrounded by magnificent old trees and manicured lawns. Buildings constructed of light colored brick bordered the area. We looked into the church, actually called a basilica, and found a cathedral with an ornate ceiling and luminous stained glass windows. We drove by the football stadium and saw "Touchdown

It was also known as the Wayne Street Historical District. We found dozens of homes built by the firm, including an especially attractive one that had housed the company architect, H. R. Stapp. The homes were charming, well maintained, individually designed and used a lot of masonry, both brick and stone. Many even had slate roofs. We took pictures, talked to people on the street, gazed in a few windows and had a wonderful time. One woman even invited Nancy in to look at her home.

cally when a ditch he was digging had collapsed on him and a friend, killing them both.

We drove back into the downtown area to the library. We found several articles on Leslie Whitcomb and his firm, and several other articles on two additional relatives who had both been governors of Indiana. In one of the articles on Leslie, Nancy's great-grandfather, we discovered the address of the family home in South Bend. Off we went.

The house at 557 Edgewater was owned by a single woman, Tina Assimos. She answered the door in her bare feet – after Nancy rang her doorbell at least four or five times. I was ready to walk away after the first two rings, but Nancy persisted. We told Tina about our search for Nancy's roots and our bike adventure along the Lincoln Highway. She listened, became somewhat comfortable

Nancy visits her great grandfather Whitcomb's home in South Bend. Right: Tina Assimos and Nancy in the living room.

Tom Evans, who saw us walking past his house with the historical district book in our hands, introduced himself and ended up featured in Nancy's video, pointing to the house where the baseball coach for Notre Dame lived.

We returned to the cemetery and discovered that indeed there were Whitcombs buried there. We found eight ancestors lying side by side. Leslie had married a second time after his first wife, Nancy's great-grandmother, had died. The two wives flanked him, one on either side. Leslie's sister, her husband and their fifteen year old son were also there. The son had died tragi-

with us, and finally allowed us to come in and look around the lower floor of the beautiful old home. The living room had a brick fireplace at the far end, and a view to the front through a screened porch, of the St. Joseph River across the street. The small kitchen still had the original wood cabinets, looking restrained and exceptionally plain, next to the new refrigerator and range. The only other concession to progress was a double stainless steel sink.

We hurried back to Plymouth for a quick lunch at the Wood Duck cafe. It was decorated with decoys and served good bean soup and homemade noodles with beef. While admiring the well preserved main street, I met a local Rotarian, a nice looking woman who was preparing for a Rotary pancake breakfast the next day. She invited me to the event, but I declined. I had to get back on the road heading east.

I finally managed to start biking at two-thirty and rode a little over forty miles under nearly perfect conditions. I was on an old piece of the highway with light traffic, warm sunny weather and a small town about every five miles. First came Inwood, then Bourbon, followed by Etna Green and Atwood. I stopped for a minute in Bourbon, and a guy who was missing two upper front teeth offered to buy me something to drink that would really get me energized for my long ride. I declined.

The final town of the day was Warsaw, a county seat and the only town on my afternoon's journey with more than 500 residents. I admired the courthouse, but

Scenes from Warsaw.
Far left: The county courthouse.
Above left: The interior of Cindy's, a classic diner.
Below left: A remnant of the Lincoln Highway.

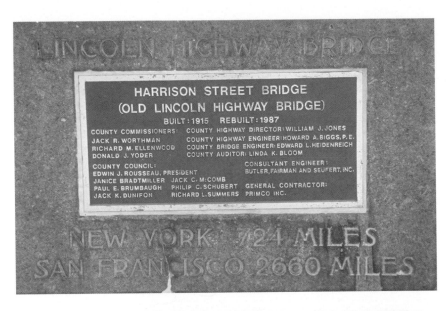

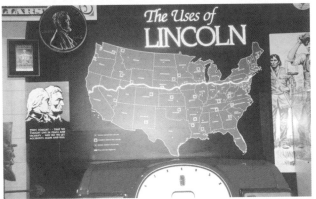

Above: A sign on a 1915 bridge across the St. Joseph River in Ft. Wayne indicates that New York is 721 miles. Below: The interior of the Lincoln Museum in Ft. Wayne.

passed through quickly, hurrying east, trying to cover as many miles as I could before Nancy caught up with me. She picked me up at a junction late in the afternoon. About six-thirty we checked into Yogi Bear's Camp Jellystone, a few miles northwest of Columbia City. I don't think I ever imagined myself staying at a place endorsed by Yogi Bear.

July 15 - Day 47
Columbia City to Van Wert, Ohio
63.7 miles

The temperature and humidity began rising soon after the sun, and then came Ft. Wayne. Riding through a city of a 100,000 or more residents is never much fun. Drivers are less patient, less tolerant, and in a bigger hurry than their country cousins. Road conditions vary from block to block and, occasionally, I took to the sidewalk or even pulled off the road to avoid a crush of vehicles. They came in waves, or packs, from behind red lights. The trick was to find a safe harbor until they passed or until road conditions improved. The Harrison Street bridge, which led into the center of the city across the St. Joseph River, had a block of granite mounted in the southern railing inscribed, "Lincoln Highway Bridge, 1915. New York - 734. San Francisco - 2660." More good news; I was getting closer.

I met Nancy at the Lincoln Museum, a new facility featuring the life and achievements of Abraham Lincoln. We watched two short films and were impressed with the exhibits. Many of them were interactive, but the concepts seemed complicated and were difficult to understand. If we were having trouble with them, what would a third grader do?

We had lunch at Cindy's Diner, a stainless steel classic box, right out of the fifties. There were sixteen stools at the counter and a narrow aisle that squeezed between the seated patrons and the exterior windows. The kitchen was in full view on the other side of the counter. A cook and two waitresses crowded past each other, back and forth, maintaining a constant dialogue with the customers. Listening to them call in their orders was a treat: "Burger with breath" (hamburger with onions); "Scorch the dog and drag it through the garden" (grilled hot dog with relish); "Beans to go" (coffee to go); "Nervous pudding" (jello); and "Leaves in the hail" (iced tea).

Two paramedics, who were obviously regular customers, were giving the cook a hard time because he refused to give them any bacon on their burgers. The youngest, and smallest, waitress was threatening to throw these two burly guys out and everyone was joining in the fun. Nancy, never very shy, began telling one of the paramedics about our adventure and the conversation soon shifted to the bike ride. The pork tenderloin sandwiches were good, but the fellowship was even better. We were even asked to sign their guest book before we left. As I paid our bill, the waitress asked, "Need some lumber?" I gave her a bewildered look and she pointed at the counter. "Oh, toothpicks. Thanks."

I crossed into Ohio in the middle of a scorching, sweaty afternoon. Nancy picked me up an hour later in Van Wert at a drive-in restaurant with an active car hop— a young male for a change. The drive-in had an extended canopy area, with several parked cars, that stretched out from a small kitchen building. In front, on the highway, was a six foot sign shaped like a giant mug of root beer. I ordered a large cold glass of the sparkling liquid before heading out to the camp.

We barbecued chicken and waited for the inside of our motor home to cool down. The humidity was oppressive. In Ohio, we were on eastern daylight time, the

Above: An old motel with night lights welcoming travelers. Below: Fireworks stand on the state border of Indiana and Ohio.

same time zone as New York City. More evidence of progress and another small victory.

*To travel hopefully is a better
thing than to arrive, and the
true success is to labor.*

—Robert Louis Stevenson

CHAPTER NINE
Ohio

July 16 - Day 48
Van Wert to Lima
39.1 miles

The first noise I heard when I awoke was the cooing of a mourning dove, followed by a chorus of other bird songs. The tranquility of our camp in the forest was exceptional, but it lasted for only five minutes before a thunderous grinding noise started, startling Nancy awake. The noises continued, first a low whirring sound, then loud groans, more whirring, and a grinding roar. We finally determined that a tree service was feeding cuttings into a wood chipper. Soon the whine of chain saws provided harmony and confirmed our diagnosis. Time to get up.

I was tired again, no energy, lethargic, sluggish. I was weary – weary of riding, weary of humidity and weary of miles of flat land covered with corn fields. The Midwest seemed to be succeeding in wearing me down where the mountains of the West had failed. The day after day effort of loading up and moving on, struggling to get everything done, being concerned about the route and what might lie ahead, was becoming more difficult. I needed an intermission. I needed a rest.

We parked just off Main Street in Van Wert. As we

were getting out of the motor home an energetic old man wearing shorts and a T-shirt walked by. He craned his neck, looked at our California licence plate and turned to ask, "Do you need help finding anything?" "No, we're just looking around," we replied. "Well, this is pretty good town to look around in," he said. "Most days anyway. Friday and Saturday nights aren't so good. That's when all those cruisers come to town. Cars are jammed bumper to bumper all the way up and down Main Street. I suppose ten percent of them are local. The rest come from all over the area, as far away as Lima." We could see why they came to Van Wert. It was a town where time seemed to have stood still for the last sixty or seventy years. There was a Second Empire courthouse on Main Street and many other buildings built before the turn of the century. There was even an active drive-in movie theater on the west side of town.

We had lunch at Balyeat's Coffee Shop, the most famous cafe in town and a Lincoln Highway landmark since 1922. Their sign in front advertised "Young Fried Chicken Day and Night." We both ordered iced tea and

Above: Landmark Balyeat's Coffee Shop.
Facing page: Early road grader.

The well preserved Main Street in Van Wert – a place where time seems to have stood still.

think of when you heard the words "fast food." It remains a safe, unchanging refuge on a famous road that no longer really exists.

The Lincoln Highway between Van Wert and Delphos is a wonderful piece of the old road with wood fences, white painted barns, and small groves of ancient maples and oaks near homes or farms. I rode past a private school with an elaborate gated entrance, the Ridge Cemetery, Conran's Better Truck Stop with a half dozen eighteen-wheeled brutes resting out in front, and an old dutch wind mill connected to one-story buildings on either side. The dutch mill must have, at one time, been a cafe connected to a garage. The road followed a ridge – the shoreline of a prehistoric version of Lake Erie – meandering through the countryside, curving gradually back and forth. A series of rectangular signs read, "Pass the – schoolhouses slow. Let the – little shavers – grow. Burma Shave." Mike Buettner, who was my Ohio Lincoln Highway expert and guide, called this section his favorite piece of the highway in Ohio. It was easy to see why.

I rode past a dead goose lying in the middle of the road. On my trip, I passed road kill frequently. I detoured around smaller birds and lots of varmints like squirrels, skunks, raccoons, possums, badgers, prairie dogs, coyotes, gophers, rabbits, frogs, woodchucks and mice. Out west I even rode by deer and antelope that weren't quite able to escape their fate while crossing the road, but it was hard to envision the circumstances that had brought a goose onto the highway.

I survived the ride into the larger city of Lima, but could not locate Nancy – I thought we had agreed to meet at the Courthouse Square. My cell phone was not working in this part of Ohio. I waited next to the courthouse for over an hour, and eventually decided that something was wrong. I hoped she was not lost or in

the baked chicken special served with corn, mashed potatoes, gravy, bread and butter. Our total bill was $10.65. We arrived shortly after eleven and, fifteen minutes later, the restaurant was nearly full. At lunch time the place became a community center with business people, retired couples, farmers and even a couple of tourists enjoying the good food.

"Mighty warm out there today," was the standard greeting. "Stay out of the heat now," the customers were advised when they left. Balyeat's didn't look like it had changed at all in the last few decades. Our food arrived quickly, but this restaurant might be the last place you'd

trouble. I found a pay phone and gave her cell phone a call. She answered and said, "Where are you?"

"I'm at the Courthouse Square," I answered. "Where are you?" She didn't answer, but I could hear her ask someone where the courthouse was located. "Stay on the phone, right where you are," she commanded. I waited and listened, as Nancy continued to talk to me. Seconds later, she appeared and waved at me. She had been waiting just a block south, on the "Lima Town Square." Well, courthouse square and town square do seem a lot alike. One more crisis vanquished.

We found a large camp with a small fenced lake that looked more like an enormous swimming pool. It was filled with kids. In these large camps, golf carts were used to visit the store, pool, golf course or the more remote neighbors, and were often driven by twelve year olds. The trailers parked in the camp appeared to be permanent with attached porches and decks, and were obviously used as vacation homes.

That evening we drove into town to meet Mike and Tammy Buettner and their two gorgeous, energetic kids, Michaela and Michael. I wanted to thank Mike for everything he had done for me, marking up all his Lincoln Highway maps across Ohio to guide me away from the most dangerous roads and to all the best landmarks in the state. Mike, who graduated from Purdue, is a consulting engineer in Lima. We had spoken on the phone, but this was our first meeting. We found an ice cream parlor and shared stories, discussing the route. Mike gave me more contacts to use on the rest of my ride through Ohio.

July 17 - Day 49
Lima to Upper Sandusky
51.7 miles

Another hot humid day, under a hazy, sweltering sky. It was still early, before nine in the morning, and heat was already raining down from the heavens, pouring like warm, thick molasses onto the roadway. It impeded my progress, puddled on the asphalt, and splashed up onto my exposed skin. The air felt more like a fluid than a gas as I swam along through the baking countryside. I envisioned my tires melting, becoming black pools of rubber on the pavement.

My first discovery of the day was curious. "High Street FREE WILL Baptist Church," proclaimed the sign in front of the modest, one-story, white building that displayed a simple wooden cross over the door. Two additional arrow-shaped signs on posts along the road had the word "REVIVAL" painted on them. They both pointed to the building. A young couple worked in front of the small house next door, the man mowing the grass and the woman weeding in the flower beds. I didn't stop, but I wondered later as I rode away what story I might have been able to tell if I had.

Ada is the home of Ohio Northern University, a teacher's college run by the Methodist Church. A woman, probably a student, was watering the flower beds at the entrance gate in front of a half-dozen attractive, brick and stone buildings that comprised the campus. In the center of town, there was a restored railroad depot and an old red caboose. In the

Nancy with Mike and Tammy Buettner and their children, Michaela and Michael.

Above: A gravestone for a bicyclist/newspaper man.
Below: Bill lights a campfire.

park next door there was a huge cannon resting on a monument with 1861-1865 inscribed above the words, "In Memory of Our Soldiers." It was the first Civil War monument I had seen on the trip and another sign that the east coast was no longer that far away.

At the Washington Township Cemetery I stopped to examine some ancient weathered gravestones. There were many I couldn't read, but one was a memorial to a little girl. The eroded, three-foot high, obelisk-shaped stone was inscribed, "ELIZA L., dau. of J. & M. Houseman, died Dec. 3, 1858. Aged 4 y 9 m 23 d." A sleeping lamb was carved over the inscription. I looked at the date and thought, "The Christmas of 1858 would not have been very merry for that family."

In Dunkirk, I stood in line inside a small convenience store, to buy a cold bottle of iced tea. In front of me, a high school kid was carefully holding seventeen dollars in quarters and dimes in his cupped hands to pay for his gasoline. He also wanted the clerk to take a package of Marlboro cigarettes out to his buddy in the car. He was underage; the guy in the car wasn't. The clerk declined, shaking her head and rolling her eyes. By the time he finished, I had an additional six people in line behind me. As I waited next to the cashier, I noticed a bulletin board with an advertisement offering AKA boxer puppies for sale and a flyer with pictures of a fourteen year old girl who had run away from home.

Coming into Upper Sandusky, I rode past an old brick factory with a rusty metal roof, surrounded by several large round brick kilns with tall chimneys, some falling apart in ruin. It served as a reminder that I was in the "Rust Belt." In the forties and fifties this was America's industrial heartland – the engine that propelled the nation's economy. Today, much of the industry is gone, leaving empty buildings and deserted, decaying downtowns. I saw signs, both in town and while riding in the country, that advertised auction sales, scheduled in the near future to dispose of properties that would not sell any other way. Lima had lost a huge locomotive works and had dropped in population from 52,000 to 42,000 in the last ten years. Growth was the major issue in our California town as well. It appeared that our problem – too much growth – was preferable to the one here – too little.

Our camp was only a few miles out of town and I wasted little time getting into the pool, decreasing my body temperature by a dozen degrees. I swore that the water hissed and steamed around me when I first lowered myself into the deep end. After dinner I wrote, Nancy walked and we both watched an unusual evening event, a hay ride around the camp celebrating Christmas in July. Twinkle lights were strung from the awning of the trailer next to us and a small Christmas tree with lights sat on their picnic table. Down the road two wooden reindeer with red bows around their necks were illuminated by a spot light. Lawn decorations, no less. Children were receiving presents and there were desserts in the game room.

We gathered branches for a bonfire, set up our folding chairs and watched the sky turn from orange to pink. Soon the lightning bugs began their nightly promenade, as they flickered and flittered across the forest floor. All that was missing was the marshmallows.

July 18 - Day 50
Upper Sandusky to Jeromesville
53.8 miles

I rode into Leesville on another of those special sections of the old road that I will remember when I think about this trip – winding, narrow, nearly deserted, a beautiful way to spend a Sunday morning. Leesville was also quiet. I found the J & M Trading Post closed. It is owned by Joe Everly, a real Lincoln Highway buff. I was looking forward to talking with Joe and finding out what I should look for on the road ahead. Nancy arrived a half hour later and worked her magic, finding Joe and his wife and getting him to open his antique store. She enjoyed their company for nearly an hour.

Just outside of Leesville there was a monument to Col. William Crawford, a lifelong friend of George Washington, who was captured by Delaware Indians near there. He was later burned at the stake for an attack his troop had made against the Indians. This attack occurred before Crawford became the commander or even a member of the troop. It didn't seem fair, but the interesting thing to me was the date, June 7, 1782.

Mansfield was recovering nicely from the loss of industry experienced by this part of the country. It had a wonderful old carousel in the center of the city that attracted families downtown. I met Nancy, who had already purchased two carousel tickets. We had lunch nearby, but were disappointed that several attractive shops in the area, including a bookstore, the Coney Island Diner and a newsstand, were closed on Sunday. We returned to the carousel and took our ride on adjacent horses, racing along, rising and falling, finishing in a dead heat.

Just west of Mansfield, after two and a half states of relatively flat country, the road began to rise upward in front of me. On the other side of town, the transition of the landscape continued. I was on huge rolling hills, climbing again, preparing for the Allegheny Mountains of western Pennsylvania. Large lakes and wooded hills replaced farm land, and I welcomed the change of scenery. It felt good to think I was finally out of the Midwestern corn fields after several weeks. It began to rain, just a sprinkle at first, then lightly for about twenty minutes, dropping the temperature to eighty degrees, reducing the difficulty of the big ascents.

I finished my day and met Nancy. We drove ahead a few miles to spend the night at a hotel in Wooster, the home of a university with the same name. We had dinner at a Greek restaurant and met Spiro, the owner, who was performing that evening in a local light opera company production of "The Student Prince." Pictures of Spiro in previous productions dating back dozens of years covered the walls. Many of the cast and the director of the orchestra – the maestro himself – were dining at the restaurant. Spiro encouraged us to attend, but we declined in favor of a night at "home."

Left: Downtown Wooster.
Right: A mural celebrates high school football in Massillon – A Century of Heros.

July 19 - Day 51
Jeromesville to East Rochester
63.7 miles

A man with a full white beard, twelve inches long, wearing a long-sleeved shirt buttoned to the neck, and a vest, also completely buttoned, sat across the dining room from us at breakfast in the hotel. His wife was dressed in a full-length pink dress with a matching shawl. The old-fashioned style of her garment suggested that she had made the outfit herself. Her hair was covered with a bonnet made of white gauze. They looked out of place, like they had walked into our lives from an earlier time. They were Mennonites. We learned that there are many of them living in this area of Ohio.

After breakfast, Nancy drove me back west of Wooster to the point I had stopped the evening before. The road into the city was great, situated in some beautiful countryside with rolling hills. It had light traffic, a good surface, and a significant climb every few miles. The lack of traffic created a problem. It allowed people to leave their dogs loose. When the road was busy – full of trucks and other vehicles – dogs were usually confined inside a fence or tied up. On this stretch of road, several dogs barked and a few gave chase. But I was still surprised and badly frightened when a large dog charged my bike. I hadn't seen the animal coming until it was nearly on top of me. My first reaction was to freeze, bracing for the impending disaster. A huge jolt of adrenaline rushed through my body. The brute began snarling

and growling, setting my heart and respiration racing. It was huge – a mangy, long-haired, yellow beast – big enough to be a small lion. It caught me easily and I was sure it was going to remove my right foot or knock me off my bike, but it turned at the last moment and ran next to me, within inches of my leg. I began pedaling like mad and pointed my finger at the creature, screaming "stay" and "down" over and over. I don't, however, think my hysterical voice turned him back. He chased along beside me until he was convinced I was leaving his territory. These episodes never failed to increase my average speed.

As I entered Massillon, I rode by a small sign that said, "Massillon Tigers, 21 Time State Champions." Impressive, I thought, but it seemed a relatively modest way of recognizing such a significant accomplishment. In the center of town all modesty was gone. At the principal intersection of the city, there was a small, well-tended park that provided the entrance garden for a two-story mural celebrating the glories of Massillon Tiger football. It depicted a triumphal arch with the words "1894 – A Century of Heroes – 1994" carved across the top. The marching band, with trombones and trumpets in front, was memorialized on the left side of the mural, just above a pantheon of gallant coaches including the legendary Paul Brown and Earl Bruce (a former Iowa State coach). On the right were the fans and the valiant tiger mascot. Heroic football players, two or three times life-sized, one black, the other white, flanked the arch in the upper portion of the masterwork. The centerpiece was a scene from the gridiron that portrayed a fall afternoon under a sky with a few white clouds. The stands were full, the action intense and the quarterback was looking down field, avoiding a heavy rush. Under this scene were the words,

"In the beginning when the great creator was drawing plans for this world of ours, he decided there should be something for everyone. He gave us mountains that reached to the sky, deep blue seas, green forests, dry deserts, gorgeous flowers and gigantic trees. Then he decided there should be football and he gave us Massillon. He created only one Massillon. He knew it would be enough."

It was hard for me to believe that the designer of this monument to high school football had done all this with a straight face, but it probably brought tears to the eyes of the passionate local fans.

Massillon Tiger souvenirs displayed in a cafe on Lincoln Way.

Top: Nancy outside the Professional Football Hall of Fame in Canton. Bottom: Hall of Fame display.

Across the street at a cafe called 49 Lincoln Way, I had lunch and learned more about high school football in this part of the country. One wall near my table had a floor to ceiling display of orange Tiger paraphernalia over twenty feet in length. Banners, cushions, caps, cups, posters, tickets, old schedules and scores, pictures and clippings made up the display; it went on endlessly. Massillon recently played McKinleyville high school of Canton for the one hundredth time. The stadiums in both cities hold over forty thousand people and they frequently fill them. When the Cleveland Browns moved to Baltimore, it would have been felt keenly in this rabid football area. I learned that their recent return was wildly celebrated. Browns and Cleveland Indian logos and flags were a constant part of the landscape as I rode through the countryside.

I met Nancy in Canton and we drove to the Professional Football Hall of Fame, across the road from the McKinleyville High School field. They hold the annual Hall of Fame game here, the first pro football exhibition of the year. The Hall of Fame Museum was great. A gift shop and cafe were downstairs. Upstairs were exhibits describing the history of the game, including a Jim Thorpe jersey and the coat he had worn in the Olympic Games when he won the decathlon. Each team had an exhibit, with Rice, Montana and Young featured in the 49er section. Another area provided highlights from every Super Bowl. Finally there were the bronze busts of all the players that had been inducted. They filled two U-shaped rooms, lining both sides of the aisle. Bill Walsh, Joe Namath and many of the old Packers, including Jim Taylor, Bart Starr, Paul Horning, Ray Nitschke and Vince Lombardi, were among the names I remembered. This area of the country concedes that it is not as crazy about football as Texas or Oklahoma, but I would have to see it to believe it.

We have been camping most nights, but it would be an exaggeration to say that we were roughing it. The camp we found on this particular day, however, was certainly not deluxe. A long bumpy gravel road led up a steep hill to the office. We were met by a fellow that promised hot showers, flush toilets and a nice level camp site. The showers were warm at best and required me to hang onto a chain to start water flowing through the nozzle. I pulled the chain to get wet; then soaped up and pulled again to rinse off. Our motor home, in our "level camp site," had a ten or fifteen degree list, making everything from eating to doing dishes and walking around a bit of a challenge. The refrigerator door closed easily however. Oh, the flush toilets. They were located two blocks away from our front door. Despite our difficulties, I decided that traveling by motor home was not that bad. Nancy loved it and was already planning her next trip.

July 20 - Day 52
East Rochester to Beaver, PA
52.4 miles

I skipped breakfast, deciding instead to have a meal in a historic tavern ten miles up the road in Hanoverton. When I arrived in the small town, I had trouble finding the tavern located a few blocks off the main road. It was built in 1837 and would have fit right into Williamsburg, Virginia. Two women were washing windows and I asked them if I could get something to eat. "Not right now," they said. "Lunch won't be served until 11:30. You'd be welcome to wait inside and have a look around." I told them that I was riding the Lincoln Highway in Ohio and a friend had suggested I visit the Spread Eagle Tavern. I also told them I didn't think my

Interior of the Spread Eagle Tavern, built in 1837.

schedule would allow me to wait an hour.

I definitely wanted to take a look around, so I went in and was introduced to the manager who, after some consultation with the kitchen staff, offered me soup and any of the sandwiches on the menu. Perfect, I thought. The upper floors of the tavern were a wonderful bed and breakfast inn. The lower floors had seven dining rooms, all spectacularly decorated. Two of the rooms had huge fireplaces, one with a mammoth elk head above it. Wood planks, eighteen inches wide, covered the floor of another room. Photos of famous republicans like Reagan, Bush and Kemp were on the walls and there was even a bust of Reagan on the mantle over one of the fireplaces. The owner was obviously active in party politics in the area. My food came and it was delicious. It felt a little strange to be the only one eating in the entire place. The manager, one of the cooks and two of the waitresses were curious about my trip. They gathered around me and we talked as I ate. One of them even telephoned the local newspaper, but I wasn't going to be around long enough to meet with their reporter. When I asked for my check, the waitress said, "The man-

across the Ohio River in Chester, West Virginia. He also called the local newspaper and a reporter soon arrived to interview Nancy and me and take my picture. Promising to send us a copy of the article, Randy shook hands with both of us and gave Nancy a Fiestaware pitcher.

Left: The rolling hills of eastern Ohio. Right: Another landmark, the Ohio River, with a bridge from East Rochester to West Virginia.

ager told me that your meal was on the house." My bike ride had earned me another meal.

I stopped after lunch to read another historical marker and learned about the Ohio River–Lake Erie canal. It was constructed in 1850, connecting the two bodies of water. It required Irish workmen to blast two long tunnels through the hills I was riding over. The canal was abandoned not long after it was completed, when the railroads penetrated into this part of the country. My favorite road sign was a yellow one. It displayed the silhouette of a truck sitting on an inclined plane. Underneath were the words, "Trucks use lower gear." For me, it meant a nice long, steep down hill run.

I found Nancy in East Liverpool in front of the antique mall. The owner, Randy, was a large friendly fellow who was also a member of the city council. He encouraged us to visit the Homer Laughlin pottery factory

We drove across the river to visit the factory, where Fiestaware is still made. For people who love and collect this pottery, this factory outlet is nirvana. The showroom had new, perfect pieces with prices that were a half to a third of what Nancy had seen in stores. Four five-piece place settings were sixty-five dollars. The treasure hunt, however, was in a large room next door – Fiestaware heaven – where there were crates and boxes and stacks of "seconds" piled randomly the length of the room – literally thousands of pieces. They were not priced, but a chart with drawings on the wall allowed you to determine the cost. A dinner plate, for instance, was two dollars. The challenge was to find a piece that wasn't badly chipped or otherwise marred, that matched the piece you had already found. Nancy was beside herself. She knew there were bargains everywhere she looked, but how many could she justify hauling home with us? The answer turned out to be three medium-sized boxes.

We drove back to East Liverpool and I took off up the Ohio River, planning to meet Nancy in Beaver, Pennsylvania. I had reached another new state and the Ohio River – two more significant milestones. Riding along the river was great, even enlightening. Tug boats pushed gigantic barges up the river. Huge factories and a big refinery were lined up between the railroad and the water. A few miles further along there was a town with homes looking out over the water to the wooded hills on the other side. More industry, more houses and then, across the river, I saw three massive cylindrical chimneys that marked the Beaver Valley Power Station, a large nuclear power plant. Steam and smoke streamed toward the sky producing a striking scene.

The road wasn't great, but I survived and arrived to find that Nancy had secured us a room in a bed and breakfast inn for the night. Jim and Sue Todd were the owners and managers of this operation, conducted in a home built in 1875. Right next door was another wonderful large old house built five years later. In that house, the Todds lived upstairs, with Jim's funeral home business downstairs.

An impressive sight – smoke and steam escaping the Beaver Valley Power station.

There is a destiny that makes us brothers
None goes his way alone.
All that we send into the lives of others
Comes back into our own.

—Edward Markham

CHAPTER TEN
Pennsylvania

July 21 - Day 53
Beaver to Irwin
53.1 miles

A special day. We were scheduled to pick up our son Eric at the airport at 3:30. I would have a riding companion across the rest of Pennsylvania. We had not seen him since the first of June and were looking forward to the reunion. First, however, I needed to ride through Pittsburgh – twenty-seven miles into the center of town and twenty-seven miles out.

I started for the city around 9:30, my mind filled with concerns about the road and what I might find on the way. After a good night's sleep, I felt ready – alert and strong. Road conditions, especially in the east, change continually. Change is the one thing a cyclist can rely on; nearly perfect conditions or even terrible conditions rarely last for more than a few minutes.

LIBERTY BRIDGE AND SKYLINE   PITTSBURGH, PA.   3

Most of the time during the ride into the city, I was on a four lane road. Sometimes the highway had a shoulder and frequently the shoulder was paved, but occasionally I was riding on the white line with a steel guard rail only inches from my right leg with traffic passing just a few feet to my left. Those times were not good. If there was any good news, it was that the traffic was light and the grades along the Ohio River were infrequent and gradual. With two lanes for traffic coming up behind me, I was usually able to ride on the edge of the pavement and have traffic pass in the far left lane. Traveling through towns was more difficult, and I often found myself riding on a narrow street with a curb. If a pack of trucks and cars ap-

Left: An old post card view of Pittsburgh.
Facing page: The mighty Ohio River, lined with industry and railroads, with the towers of Pittsburgh visible in the upper left.

proached from behind, I would turn into a driveway off the road, and ride on the sidewalk until they passed. Given the poor conditions, it went fairly well. I either felt safe, or I moved off the road and waited for the traffic to clear. After twenty-seven miles of following the river, I reached the confluence (I love that word!) of the Allegheny and Monongahela Rivers – the beginning of the Ohio River. I passed by Three Rivers Stadium and rode across the bridge, toward the forest of office towers, into the city of Pittsburgh.

Eric joins his dad for the trip across Pennsylvania.

As soon as I arrived, I pulled over and called Nancy, informing her of my safe arrival. She was on her way to visit the Andy Warhol Museum. I continued on my way, trying to leave as much of the urban area behind before meeting Nancy and driving to the airport to pick up Eric. My route through and out of town had been charted by Bill Hoffman, a cyclist from Lancaster, Pennsylvania, whom I found via the Internet. The route was dramatically better than the roads I had followed into the city. It allowed me to ride in relatively safe conditions, following along a rail line out of town,

avoiding many hills in an extremely hilly city.

In the city, the neighborhood along Liberty Street was attractive, with a lively commercial area and even a few bicycle riders. I thought about stopping for lunch but pedaled on. Several miles later I reached Braddock, along the Monongahela side of the city. I entertained no thoughts about stopping here. "Historic Braddock," as one sign proclaimed, was a scary neighborhood populated by derelicts, with boarded-up windows, broken pavement, and decaying buildings. If someone told me this area was the site of a long civil war, I would believe them. It was a bombed out, burned up scene.

I thought I would never get out of Pittsburgh, but I finally found a group of stores that signaled the suburbs: K-mart, Wendy's, McDonald's and Pier One, all within the space of a mile. I was near Greensburg when I finally rendezvoused with Nancy about 2:30. She was not happy. Pittsburgh had been a nightmare for the driver of a twenty-four foot motor home. She couldn't find her way out of town and then was nearly run off the road a time or two.

She had not eaten lunch and I could tell she was steaming when she walked into a mini-mart to buy us sandwiches. I quickly changed clothes and listened to her tale of woe as she drove to the airport while I navigated.

We arrived fifteen minutes before Eric's flight. After

belief that my power and invulnerability resided in my unshorn locks. My clothes seem to have grown larger while my hair has grown longer. Pants were hanging loosely around my waist that were tight when we left California. Aches and pains of the early weeks of the trip had vanished and I felt better than I had in years. It's a rather radical prescription for good health, but riding a bike every day for six or seven weeks seems to be a special kind of tonic. Even my allergies had disappeared somewhere in western Nebraska. At least there was one advantage of the very high humidity we had.

An elaborate tower dominates a railrosad station in Greensburg.

our happy reunion, we drove back into the city to tour the Shadyside neighborhood of the city and visit Carnegie Mellon University. Parking was impossible, so I finally pulled into an area reserved for university buses and stayed with the motor home while Nancy and Eric toured the campus. We made a fleeting attempt to see some of the rest of Pittsburgh, but I was exhausted, as well as hungry. We quickly gave up and drove the turnpike back to Greensburg where we were able to secure the last room at a Holiday Inn. The Honeymoon Suite had a king bed for Nancy and I and a sofa bed in the living room for Eric. We fit perfectly.

I had not cut my hair since the day we left on the fourth of June, and I did not plan to cut it until after I reached New York City. I had acquired a Samson-like

July 22 - Day 54
Irwin to Somerset
54.4 miles

We were not in a hurry in the morning. I caught up with my journal and allowed Eric a chance to sleep in and adjust to the three-hour time difference. Eric is twenty-seven and a graduate of UCLA. He's a self-employed contractor, building houses in Davis. He rides his bike occasionally, but keeps in shape playing basketball. The pavement was wet when we walked out to the motor home, carrying our belongings in our hands. Visits to motels were a challenge without luggage. Nancy used a shopping bag and I used my briefcase, my pockets and my hands. We always seemed to forget one or two things in the motor home, necessitating second and third trips.

Our road was fine and Eric and I made good time riding into Greensburg, working hard as we climbed hill after hill. The fifteen miles passed quickly for me because of the company. There was a railroad station, built just after the turn of the century, that we couldn't resist. We stopped to take a few pictures of its tower and other elaborate decorations. After a cold drink, we continued out of town, pushing the pace as much as possible, trying to make up for our late start. We wanted to visit Fallingwater, Frank Lloyd Wright's most famous house, located just nineteen miles south of our route.

As we rode farther away from Greensburg, we found more hills and fewer people, beautiful mountain scenery. I became worried that we had missed our last opportunity for lunch when we rolled through a small crossroads neighborhood that had no services of any kind. Three miles later we entered Pleasant Unity, located, of course, at the top of difficult climb. We soon located the Country Cafe and Video Store. We turned off the road and parked our bikes. As we were taking off our helmets, a couple on their way into the cafe stopped to ask about our bikes and the riding conditions around here. We followed them into the full cafe and allowed them to sit down at the last empty table.

We looked around for a minute and I noticed a gray-haired lady staring up at me. She caught my eye and said, "How tall are you?" "Six-foot four," I answered. "No, you're taller than that. My nephew is six-foot seven and you are at least as tall as he is." I had Eric assure her that I had indeed given her the correct height. She invited us to join her and the man sitting next to her at their table. The couple that we had followed into the cafe then called out to us, "Oh, we wanted you to sit with us." Since we were already in our chairs, we thanked them and stayed where we were. It turned out that the lady we had joined was famous. "A few years ago," she explained, "I entered a county-wide age-group paddle boat race with a friend of mine and we not only won but set a record, a record that still stands, even today. Last year I went to another state contest and came in second in shuffle board. I should have won, but I let up at the end." She was seventy-eight, almost a state champ and a great believer in the value of exercise.

Her companion was a renovation contractor who was working on her house, built around 1920. He extolled the virtues of older houses. "All the lumber is hardwood. The two by twelve rafters are actually two inches thick and twelve inches high, not an inch and a half by eleven and a quarter. The doors are solid oak, about this thick." He held his fingers maybe two inches apart. "We have been working on the outside, sanding and repairing the wood exterior. It's amazing – the oak looks new once it's sanded." We enjoyed hearing about the project and sharing some stories from our trip.

We got up to leave and several people came over to wish us well, walking with us out to our bikes. Our elderly companion grabbed my hand with both of hers and said, "The Lord be with you, William. Always put him first and you'll be fine." A twelve year old asked Eric to explain how we were able to ride on tires that were so skinny. As we rode away, eight people who had followed us outside stood waving, bidding us farewell.

The road became more difficult, the grades steeper, forcing us into our lowest "granny gear." In Lycipus a man watched me ride by and said, "Hey, I can save you guys some trouble." Since he was driving a truck I thought he was offering us a ride and I declined. "Oh, no," he said. "Highway 130, the road you're on, climbs a terrible hill. If you turn left here, you'll find Possum Hollow Road. It's a bottom road and takes you back to the highway just beyond the hill." We thanked him and took the alternate route. The road was pretty and perhaps we missed some climbing, but there was still a lot of hill remaining after we returned to the highway. It was incredibly hot and humid. During the climbs, we

traveled too slowly to generate any breeze. With no wind rushing by to cool us off, our exertion turned us into blast furnaces, radiating heat into the hot afternoon from our wet, red faces. Nancy called twice. "Where are you? I thought you'd be here by now." Too many hills. A little after three we limped into a gravel area, just off the road. We loaded our bikes onto the motor home and started south to see one of the most famous houses in the world.

We arrived in time to catch a four o'clock tour. Fallingwater and the site were both spectacular. A stream cascaded down the valley, landing on wide platforms of rock, creating two major waterfalls, about ten feet in height, and several smaller ones. The house stood on the other side of the stream, squeezed between the river and the rock wall that formed the far side of the valley.

Inside the great room, used for both living and dining, there were windows on three sides looking out to the forest and down to the stream. The fourth side was dominated by a huge fireplace sitting on a large slab of

Two views of Fallingwater, one of the most famous structures designed by Frank Lloyd Wright.

Top left: Laurel Summit.
Top right: Eric drinks after long climb through the mountains.
Bottom: A spectacular ceramic tile, Art Deco gas station in Bedford.

native rock that remained part of the mountain. The room and the decks surged out from the side of the mountain, seeming to defy gravity and float over the stream and the upper falls, with strong horizontal lines. A stair led down from inside the great room to the stream.

The bedrooms were beautiful tree house spaces above the main room, with their own decks jutting out into space, looking out into the leafy forest world. It would have been interesting to be a guest in that house for a weekend. A sunny day with light flowing in through all the windows would be wonderful – with time to bathe in the waterfall under the house. I would also have loved to experience a storm, with rain splashing off the many skylights and wind moving through the trees. The most spectacular view of Wright's masterpiece was from down below, along the river, looking up at the house soaring out over the stream and its falling water.

We returned to our route and I jumped out of the motor home and got on my bike. Eric had decided to pass on any more riding, to live to fight another day, and went with Nancy to locate a place for the night. I had hoped for a reasonably easy, fifteen mile ride. It turned out to be twenty, and began with a five mile climb in the late afternoon heat. At the top was Laurel Summit, 2,728 feet high. I was as happy to make it over that summit as I had been on any of the more lofty passes out in the west. I finished the day with a climb into Somerset and found Eric and Nancy waiting at the Holiday Inn.

July 23 - Day 55
Somerset to Breezewood
55.4 miles

When I looked out of the window early in the morning, I found it impossible to see across the street because of a thick fog. I reasoned that we might have a cool morning and was surprised at how hot and uncomfortable the temperature was a little over an hour later. Eric and I coasted down a short hill to the Summit Diner and ate breakfast, leaving Nancy to finish up some e-mail in the motel. Inside the diner we found a framed quotation. It read, "The diner is a roadside beacon, a message to the traveler that ahead there's welcome relief from tired backs and burning eyes and darkness and the tedious isolation of the highway."

We started climbing as soon as we left town. After five miles of roller-coaster roads, we started up a long hill. Sweat blossomed on my forearms, leaving a garden of droplets, as we worked our way up the hill. Seven miles out of town, we stopped in the shade to take a break and call Nancy on the cell phone. She was in the laundromat and agreed to meet us in Bedford. As I held the phone to my ear, I watched perspiration flow off my elbow. It formed a small stream, falling to the ground, creating a puddle on the asphalt near my feet. Eric and I were both wet, our jerseys and shorts thoroughly soaked. Last night, I worried about the steep slopes of the Alleghenies. I had not even considered the heat. I hoped we had fifty more miles left in us.

After a second major climb, we looked out into the distance from the crest of the mountain and saw a beautiful sight, a wide valley far below us, extending for some distance to the east. Our downhill run was long, fast and exhilarating. After the descent, the road continued gradually downhill, following the Raystown Branch of the Juniata River, allowing us to speed along with a minimum of effort. Still, we were relieved when the town of Manns Choice finally appeared. It was nearly one o'clock and we were hungry, thirsty and hot. We walked into "D's Hitching Post" and, in contrast with lunch the day before, found an empty restaurant. A woman was behind the bar, but she turned away as we appeared and, without a word, walked back into the kitchen. She seemed to be hoping we'd just go away and leave her alone in her cool, empty bar room. Not a chance. She finally returned and we ordered soup, hamburgers and fries. The food was delicious, and when we complimented our cook/waitress, she relaxed her guard and asked us where we were going. After a short conversation, we left

Above: Bill prepares for the road after breakfast at the Summit Diner.
– Eric Roe photo
Below: A gentle curve along Main Street in Everett.

A crowded off-ramp at Breezewood on the Pennsyvania Turnpike.

feeling revived and pedaled on to Bedford, once again returning to the Lincoln Highway – the highway we had left two days ago in Greensburg in search of better bike roads.

Nancy was parked along the street. We joined her and walked to a crafts fair at "the Squares." It consisted of three parks on three sides of an intersection, with the fourth side occupied by a lovely old brick courthouse. A sign announced that these squares had been given to the city by William Penn in 1763. Ten years earlier, troops had been assembled to fight against the Indians at Fort Bedford. One of the officers was a young man named George, who now appears on the face of our one dollar bills. Those early dates made my goal on the Atlantic Ocean seem almost in the neighborhood.

Forty miles were complete and the last half of the trip had been relatively easy, but I still needed to reach Breezewood to conclude my day. Eric joined Nancy in the motor home and I aimed my bike again to the east. Passing through Everett was a treat, with its great old Main Street. My favorite building was a corner cafe with a motel above, built of decorative concrete block with an old greenish sign hanging out into the street that proclaimed "Catherine's Corner, Air Conditioning and Television." A decaying old movie house named after the town and a two-story hotel also caught my attention, as did a church further down the street with a tall white steeple. It occurred to me that I would have missed this wonder-

ful downtown if I had chosen to travel by car along the Interstate. These old highways certainly didn't permit you to travel at eighty miles per hour, but they were a lot more interesting.

The fifteen miles to Breezewood were not bad, except for a construction zone. Eric had called to warn me about it from up ahead. A bridge was being repaired and two traffic lanes had been squeezed into one, allowing work on the opposite side of the road. While crossing the bridge, I had no choice but to take my entire lane. This forced the car behind me to slow down and follow me until I could completely cross the long bridge and move, once again, back onto the shoulder. Nobody honked or yelled, so I assumed they weren't terribly inconvenienced. The road climbed, once again, the last few miles before town. I hung in there, knowing that the end was near. I found Eric enjoying the pool at the motel and joined him for a dip before dinner.

July 24 - Day 56
Breezewood to Chambersburg
52.5 miles

Our attempt to leave early was thwarted by a thunderstorm. Eric and I had breakfast and started up the hill out of town a little after ten on wet pavement. Breezewood is the junction of I-70, heading south to Baltimore and Washington, D. C., and the Pennsylvania Turnpike, I-76, connecting Pittsburgh and Philadelphia. This major junction has nearly every franchise fast food restaurant, gas station and motel in existence and there was an amazing forest of highway signs, billboards and neon along the main road.

We left the signs behind and climbed Ray's Hill. On a better day, there are thirty-mile views. The distant valleys and the mountains marching away in all directions were still impressive, but I would have been pleased if there weren't quite so many to the east. We turned off Highway 30 to take a route recommended by Bill Hoffman, my Pennsylvania cycling guide. We enjoyed the back roads that ran through forestland and, unfortunately, found plenty of hills to climb. By one o'clock, we'd only ridden twenty-five miles. We had been slowed by the mountains, but the heat was unquestionably our

most serious enemy. It had seemed cooler after the morning's rain, but, after less than an hour of riding, we were back in a steam bath.

We stopped for lunch at Burnt Cabins in another bar. Yes, Burnt Cabins was the name of the town. At one time government troops had burned the cabins of the settlers in this area to appease a local Indian tribe, thus the name. I'm sure those settlers didn't appreciate being the sacrificial lambs.

We ordered cheeseburgers and fries. While we waited, Eric talked with the only other customer in the place, a guy with a long ponytail wearing an auto racing T-shirt. Posters of race cars were on the walls and a schedule of this year's NASCAR events was right behind us. Eric decided that a racing question might get a better response than one about basketball, so he asked, "Looks like Jeff Gordon did pretty well last year. Was he the NASCAR champ?" "Yeah, but he's only fourth or fifth in the Winston Cup standings this year," the guy replied. He had an unusual country accent that was difficult to understand, but we learned a little.

Back on the bikes, we enjoyed the climb up Forbes Trail, a road that took us through Cowens Gap. General Forbes established a string of forts in western Pennsylvania around 1730. Forbes Trail connected these forts, the last one being Fort Pitt, later Pittsburgh. We were following another historic trail, another road that led pioneers west. The forest arched over the roadway, creating an continuous cathedral effect with shafts of sunlight streaming down through scattered openings in the leaves. These streams of light contrasted so vividly with the darkness of the forest that they appeared to be solid, almost like pillars holding up the sky, barricades to be avoided by our bikes. The climb was gentle and the shade of the woods lowered the temperature. We were making good time when Eric lost the chain on his bike. We barely managed to pry it back in place, turning our hands into greasy black gloves. Unfortunately, something was damaged or moved out of alignment in the process, and his bike would not stay in gear. We were, however, near the top of the climb. We

A shaded section of the Forbes Trail at Cowens Gap, near Ft. Louden.
– Eric Roe photo

stopped to call our emergency number, 1-800-NANCY, and she agreed to meet us at 2:30 in Fort Louden, where our road returned to Highway 30 at the bottom of Toscarosa Hill.

I was having troubles as well. The front derailer on

Lakeside at the summit of Toscarosa Hill near Ft. Louden.

my bike would not allow me use my highest gear wheel. Nancy learned that the bike shop in Chambersburg would close at four. At the bike shop, they found that the cable leading to my handle bar from my derailer had only two strands of wire left unbroken. The other fifteen or twenty were severed and I had been close to having big problems. Eric's bike was a mess, but since he only needed it for another three days, we asked the mechanic to repair what he could. He was able to remove a link from the chain, make a few adjustments and actually left Eric with a bike that was in better shape than when he started out on it a few days earlier.

We returned fifteen miles back to Fort Louden. I needed to complete the ride into Chambersburg, while Eric went exploring with Nancy. There were still some

hills, but I was finally riding out of the eastern mountains. The Alleghenies had been more formidable than I had expected and I had expected them to be difficult. The heat and humidity had also played a role. This part of the country was experiencing a historical heat wave. Harrisburg had set four record high temperatures in July. The heat index, taking into account humidity – sort of the summer equivalent of a wind chill factor – had been consistently above one hundred and twenty degrees. Lawns, fields and orchards were suffering from the drought. The grass was brown, the corn stunted and tiny apples were lying prematurely in piles under the trees. I had hoped to be in Gettysburg by the end of the day, but after 54 miles I was in Chambersburg, twenty-six miles away from my goal.

July 25 - Day 57
Chambersburg to York
52.6 miles

Just as Eric and I were finishing breakfast at the motel, a boy, maybe six years old, walked through the dining room with his father. He looked closely at Eric, who stood up from his chair just as the boy was walking by. At six-foot three, he towered well above the child, his multicolored cycling jersey exhibiting the logos of a variety of bicycle-related products. As the boy and his dad left the room, we overheard him whisper to his father, "He's a race car driver, isn't he dad?" We smiled.

We were reminded that it was Sunday when organ music floated out through the open door of a church as we rode by, accompanied by the voices of the congregation singing a hymn. Thadeus Stevens' blacksmith shop, dated 1830, stood next to the road, a "service station" from another era. We had one more ridge to cross on our way to Gettysburg before we put the mountains completely behind us. The climb was not steep and, with our bikes newly repaired, the miles passed quickly. In the forestland at the top of the ridge, we rode in the shade of the trees. Cool air was sliding down the slope out of

the woods to our right. Eric called it "forest air conditioning." It felt wonderful, despite the fact that the temperature displayed on my speedometer had only dropped into the high seventies. Compared to the last several days it was positively frigid. My speedometer not only displayed my speed, but it also provided me with the time and temperature, my average speed, daily miles, total miles and maximum speed.

We arrived at the west side of Gettysburg just after ten thirty and found the site where fighting had occurred on the first day of the famous battle. General Robert E. Lee bivouacked in Chambersburg before moving the Army of Northern Virginia east to Gettysburg the first of July, 1863. Lee's army came down the same road we had just ridden to Gettysburg. Federal troops met the Confederates with cannon and calvary, forcing them to move north and south as they streamed, in a long line, out of the mountains from the west, trying to find a way around that pocket of resistance.

We called Nancy to tell her that we had arrived in Gettysburg and to find out when she might join us for a tour of the battlefield. She was finished with her visit to Jiffy-Lube and had the motor home headed our way. In front of a visitor center, we sat in the shade, talking with a local guide about the battle and the war. Lee and his army were in Pennsylvania looking for food and one more decisive victory. Lincoln's generals had done little, despite their huge advantages in men and material. With another loss this far north, Lincoln would have been forced to compromise with the south.

Nancy arrived and we put our bikes on the back, ready to begin the motor tour. Lee's army had ultimately compelled the union forces to retreat to an area south

Left: A farm near Gettysburg.
Right: A blacksmith shop on the road between Chambersbury and Gettysburg.

Left: Eric at the Gettysberg battlefield and a view from Little Round Top. Right: The Robert E. Lee Monument at the Gettysburg battlefield.

VIRGINIA TO HER SONS AT GETTYSBURG

ninety thousand northern troops along a five-mile line, about three-fourths of a mile apart. We drove along the ridge where the southern army had camped, stopping to look at the many monuments to the soldiers from North Carolina, Virginia, Tennessee and Mississippi. The most impressive was the tribute to Robert E. Lee. The old gentleman sat on his faithful horse Traveler on top of a two story column of stone, gazing out over the field of battle. When Lee fought at Gettysburg, he was fifty-seven years old, the same age as the old gentleman on the bicycle following the Lincoln Highway across the country.

At the southern end of the battlefield, we turned east and drove to the far end of the Union lines at Little Round Top. Much of the second day's action occurred here, as the South attempted to capture this strategic high point. Over four thousand dead were recovered from the slopes of this hill. We drove north along Cemetery Ridge to where, on the third day, Lee had ordered the offensive known as Pickett's Charge. Following two hours of the most violent exchange of artillery of the war, twelve thousand southern troops formed up in a line over a mile long and, with battle flags flying, charged across the fields to win the war for the Confederacy. One Confederate soldier, Private Shotwell, described it as follows: "The flags flutter and snap – the sunlight flashes from the officer's swords – low words of command are heard – and thus in perfect order, this gallant array of gallant men marches straight down into the valley of death."

They made it to the Union lines, but failed to sustain the foothold. Five thousand died. Grant won at Vicksburg the next day and the South was on the path that would lead them in two years to Appomattox. Over fifty thousand men were killed, wounded, or listed as missing at Gettysburg. It is impossible to visit the battlefield and not be moved by the magnificent bravery and horror of it all. As we read the materials provided by the

of town. The Union Army occupied Cemetery Ridge which ran south from the city's cemetery and ended five miles away at a rocky promontory called Little Round Top. Lee formed his army just west of them on Seminary Ridge. Seventy thousand southern troops were facing

National Parks Service and looked out over the fields, we could literally see the action that had taken place on those three fateful days in July of 1863.

We drove into town for a late lunch. Afterwards, I started biking towards York, while Nancy and Eric returned to visit the National Cemetery where Lincoln made

his famous address. In York, I rode by the Golden Plow Tavern built in 1741, using a massive rough-hewn, half-timber style – a medieval-looking building. I waited a few minutes for Nancy and Eric to arrive. We were leaving our route for an overnight vacation, a trip north to visit the city of Hershey, Pennsylvania.

The Hotel Hershey, where we stayed, was blanketed with petunias. Baskets of petunias hung from poles, and large round stone dishes of petunias sat on the balconies. Beds of petunias and other flowers flanked the entrance. As you viewed the building from a distance, pink, white and purple petunias seemed to be growing out of all the nooks and crannies of the architecture, adding a profusion of color to the large gray masonry palace.

We showered, changed clothes quickly and returned to a terrace restaurant to enjoy dinner, looking out over the rolling hills of the area. We were surrounded by fami-

lies. The Hershey Amusement Park was across the street, complete with an old fashioned wood roller-coaster. The sky gradually darkened and the clouds turned from white to wonderful shades of pink, purple and finally gray – a sunset inspired by the petunias, reflecting their colors in the clouds. We were given Hershey's chocolate bars

when we checked in, grabbed a handful of Hershey's miniatures as we left the restaurant and found several Hershey's chocolate kisses the maid left for us when she turned down our beds. Massive bouquets of flowers and mountains of chocolate, it sounded like a good idea for a hotel. For us, Hershey was literally a treat.

July 26 - Day 58
York to Lancaster
23.8 miles

We had breakfast in the Circular Dining Room, overlooking the hotel gardens outside. Inside, there was constant activity, families eating quickly, kids rushing about, excited to get over to the rides at the amusement park. After checking out, we vis-

Left: The Golden Plow Tavern in York built in 1741.
Center: Bill and Nancy at the Hershey Hotel. – Eric Roe photo
Left: Another view of the Hershey Hotel and the bountiful petunias.

Bill Roe with Bill Hoffman, his cycling guide for Pennsylvania and New Jersey.
– Eric Roe photo

ited the Hershey Museum and enjoyed the collection of Native American and Pennsylvania German articles. There was also a large collection of memorabilia from the Hershey mansion and the town. Hershey had built the high school, the city hall and many of the homes for the employees in his chocolate factory. Next door was Chocolate World. We waited in line to take a Disney-style ride past a series of exhibits that detailed all that was involved in making chocolate, combining cocoa beans from the tropics, fresh milk from local dairies and lots of sugar. The smell of chocolate was even piped in near the end of the ride – an effective touch. At the conclusion, a free candy bar for everyone.

After we returned to York on a day I had originally planned to rest, I rode the twenty-five miles to Lancaster, back on the Lincoln Highway. This made fifteen days in a row of riding. Too many, but I only had four to go. Nancy and Eric found a place to have some work done on the motor home and met me in the middle of Lancaster. Between the two cities, I crossed over the wide expanse of the Susquehanna River on an arched bridge built in 1930. The Delaware and the Hudson were about the only major obstacles that remained in my path. There were, of course, a few small hurdles that weren't rivers, namely Philadelphia, Newark and all the suburbs, and then the length of Manhattan.

We spent the rest of the afternoon looking for a town to visit north of the city. Although we missed the town, we did find quite a bit of road construction and its collateral confusion before emerging into the beautiful rolling countryside of Lancaster County. The picture perfect farms of the Amish dotted the landscape, huge old white barns next to tall silos. We stopped at a visitor's center to get our bearings and watched a fifteen minute presentation on the area. Then we called Bill Hoffman and received directions to his home. Bill is in his fifties, slender and fit. Daily bike riding has pared his body weight, leaving only the essentials necessary to power him along the road. Before he recently retired, Bill worked for a bank analyzing locations for new branches. His work required him to travel throughout the northeast, gaving him an opportunity to discover many of the best bike roads in this part of the country. The Pennsylvania Governor commissions Bill to design a route for an annual ride across the state. Bill also chairs the Pennsylvania Pedalcycle and Pedestrian Advisory Committee.

As I have traveled across the country, I have been asked by many people how I could possibly ride by myself, unprotected, at the mercy of any angry motorist or outlaw. I tell them that I always felt safe. Bill Hoffman was part of the reason I felt that way. Before I left, we spent time corresponding via the Internet, as he designed a safe path for me to take across his state and all of New Jersey. For those efforts alone, I will always be grateful. He also invited three strangers into his home, providing us with a delicious lasagna dinner, cherry pie for dessert, comfortable bedrooms and a nice hot shower.[1]

---

[1] I rode across the country and ended the year with 7,710 miles on my bike. Bill Hoffman sent me his holiday letter. He didn't ride cross-country and reported that his mileage for this year would be down to only 9,600 miles. In the decade of the nineties Bill biked 95,700 miles, ranging from a high in 1992 of 11,000 miles to 8,000 in 1993, a year he spent six weeks off his bike with a broken ankle. He has biked 228,000 miles since he "resumed serious cycling" in 1971. He hopes to reach half a million miles before he comes "to the last exit."

July 27 - Day 59
Lancaster to Paoli
55.4 miles

I had difficulty sleeping again and was up before six with a lot on my mind. I snuck down to the kitchen to catch up on my journal and was joined by Bill a half hour later. We talked and waited until eight to wake up Eric and Nancy. Bill rode his bike into the center of Lancaster and met us at the Central Market, housed in a old red brick building with gas lamps and courtly towers. It dates back to the 1730s and is the oldest covered market in the nation. Fresh fruits, home grown vegetables, baked goods, flowers, fish, cheese, meat and a variety of local crafts filled the booths. We bought some peaches and sticky buns before walking to the other side of the block for breakfast.

We discovered that Lancaster had been one of our national capitals – for one day. The Continental Congress had fled from Philadelphia when the British army advanced close to the city. After meeting for a day in Lancaster, they decided a little more distance between themselves and the advancing army might be prudent. They crossed the wide Susquehanna and spent the winter in York. This was the same winter that Washington and his army were suffering through the cold, bitter weather of Valley Forge, located a short distance northwest of Philadelphia.

Bill rode with us, guiding us out of town into the country. We took lightly traveled, two lane roads into Lancaster County, home of many Amish farmers. This was Bill's backyard. We saw a farmer with a team of mules working a field of hay. A teenaged girl came down the road in a horse drawn cart with her two younger brothers. Two boys were busy painting a fence out near the road, while three men were replacing siding on their home. The crops looked healthy and the farms, about fifty to sixty acres in size, were immaculate and orderly,

Left: An Amish farm.

Right: An old post card of Amish boys on the road near Lancaster.

"Antique Roe," a shop near Gap.

the farm yards planted with flowers. There were some wonderful scenes of rural life and I was tempted to take a few pictures. The Amish do not like to have their picture taken and many people ignore their wishes. I didn't want to be an ugly tourist, especially in front of Bill, so I left my camera in the bag.

Two Amish women and three girls sat in the shade, working on their needlework. They waved as we rode by. You could tell which farms were Amish because no power lines ran into the homes. We did notice windmills providing some power. One room schools, with a pair of outhouses, were located every few miles.

The Amish remained a mystery to me. I had some appreciation of why they decided to turn their backs on twentieth-century technologies and live without electricity, automobiles or telephones, choosing gas lamps and the horse and buggy – a less frantic, more peaceful path

through life. Riding a bike from the Pacific to the Atlantic was not the swiftest way to get from one side of the country to the other. They feel that modern conveniences can be destructive to family life. It was more difficult to understand their rejection of higher education. The children attend school until they finish the eighth grade, learning some basics: reading, writing and arithmetic; but no literature except the bible, no advanced math, science, language or higher education of any kind. The Amish core values of modesty, humility and obedience are the three virtues that inspire every decision Amish people make: the kind of clothes they wear, the way they educate their children and the kind of work they do to support their families.

I felt like I was visiting a foreign country, observing their native culture. The men were dressed alike in blue long sleeved shirts, long dark trousers – without zippers or fly – and straw hats with broad brims and a round, flat crown. The women wore long dresses, blue in color, long sleeves and gauze bonnets. A graveyard was filled with flat, round-topped gravestones, all exactly the same size and shape, all lined up in rows, all facing the same direction. The only differences in the stones we could find was the date and the lettering: some were older and some were inscribed in German, others English. In life, all men and women were equal. Now in death, no one would be superior or distinctive.

In Intercourse (that's the name of the town; I didn't make it up), we had a cold drink and waited for Nancy. Several black, squarish Amish carriages were in town, each pulled by a single, good-looking horse. Along the street, I saw children propelling themselves on scooters. I was surprised that the Amish didn't use bicycles. They seemed like such a perfect fit for them. Bill and I left town and rode the five or six miles to the town of Gap, while Eric and Nancy looked at a hardwood rocker

Eric had seen. All four of us had lunch in Gap at the Country Diner, our last meal with Bill before he turned back for home.

Gap was named for the slot in the ridge above the town that separates Lancaster County from Philadelphia and its suburbs. Amtrak passes through there, as did the Lincoln Highway and the Lancaster Pike, one of the country's first toll roads. Eric and I started our ride after lunch, climbing through the gap, the first of thirty-five more hot miles into the western fringe of Philadelphia.

We finished our ride twenty miles short of the center of the city and met Nancy at a commuter railroad station. We loaded our bikes, drove out of the parking lot and started under the railroad undercrossing to find a motel. Five feet short of the underpass, Nancy stopped in the middle of our lane. It was about six o'clock in the afternoon, rush hour. I looked at her and found her pointing at a sign warning motorists that there was only 10' 6" of clearance in the underpass. Our motor home wasn't going to make it. I jumped out, had the traffic behind us back up a bit, and eventually convinced the oncoming stream of cars in the other lane to stop. Nancy managed to back across into the other lane, and proceed backwards for half a block before backing around a corner out of harm's way. We sat there stunned, watching traffic stream by in front of us, surprised that we manage to escape the monumental traffic jam we created.

While all this was unfolding, Eric was fighting a gallant but losing battle with a broken half gallon of apple juice. The massive leak wreaked havoc inside the refrigerator and all over the floor. Nancy managed to return us to the parking lot so that Eric and I could finish cleaning up the apple cider that seemed to be everywhere.

Somewhat shaken, we once again pointed north, headed for the turnpike and a motel for the night.

A view of the Philadelphia skyline across the Schuylkill River.

July 28 - Day 60
Paoli to Princeton, New Jersey
80.7 miles

At breakfast in the hotel, we spoke with a woman from Germany who had married an American serviceman in 1958. She lived in Sacramento for a short time while her husband was posted to Korea. Pleasant and curious, she appeared interested in our trip and asked several questions. She was working at the hotel, saving her money and planning for the time when she could retire. Her husband had died many years ago and she had not been able to return to Germany since her mother died in 1964.

Nancy and Eric returned me to my route. I started down peaceful, shady Conestoga Road towards Phila-

Above left: Philadelphia's Broad Street, with a view of City Hall.
Above right: Eric pulls a wheelie in front of a South Street art project.
Lower right: Geno's Steaks in the Italian market district.

delphia. The now common noise of cicadas, chattering and rattling in the trees, applauding my efforts as I rode by. The male cicadas, like a cricket with an amplifier, produces a shrill noise by vibrating membranes on the underside of his abdomen. The cicada is about two inches long with large transparent wings.

The homes in Bryn Mawr were on large lots, sitting back from the street in groves of trees. In another five miles, the cityscape began to change and I was soon riding through a ghetto. It wasn't as scary as it was sad, but life continued. A well dressed man crossed the street, greeting a neighbor with a friendly wave. A few minutes later a women with two kids said hello and returned my smile as I rode past.

In less than an hour, I stopped halfway across the Schuylkill River and called Nancy. We had agreed to meet at the Museum of Art, but the plan had changed. Eric directed me to South Street, where they were attempting to find a place to park. Riding between the skyscrapers, down the canyon of Broad Street, Philadelphia's main thoroughfare, gave me a preview of what my ride down Broadway in two days would be like. I arrived in the South Street neighborhood in a matter of minutes, exhilarated by my ride, and asked a man with a huge handlebar mustache for directions.

I found a bakery, bought a chocolate brownie and bottle of cold orange juice, and sat down in front in the shade to savor the morning. I called Eric again and found that they were still searching for a parking place. Women walked by in their summer dresses, and I was enjoying the sights on this pleasant residential street. The man with the mustache came by on the other side of the street and shouted over to me, "You've done well. That's the best bakery in the city." Everything did taste good. It's amazing how quickly things can move from the ridiculous to the sublime. Not that long ago, we were backing out of railroad undercrossing into rush hour traffic while cleaning up apple cider; for the moment, all was right with the world.

Eric and Nancy joined me at the bakery and ordered treats. Eric and I then took off on our bikes to visit the Italian market section just to the south. This section was made famous when Sylvester Stallone, as Rocky Balboa, ran down the street training for his big fight, receiving encouragement from all the vendors along the way. There was an incredible variety of fruits, vegetables and meat. As we rode by the mountains of fresh fish, I decided it might be time to trade my beef and pork diet in for a little seafood. Near the end of the market were two extraordinary-looking restaurants, both selling the famous Philly steak sandwiches. The two buildings faced each other, both fitting into triangles formed by intersecting streets. Garish signs covering the exterior of the structures competed for your attention. Sidewalk tables surrounded the buildings, and at 11:30 they were beginning to fill with patrons.

We joined Nancy and decided we needed to sample one of these famous sandwiches. We went to Jim's Steaks at 400 South Street and stood waiting in line with fifteen or twenty people next to the kitchen, a symphony of shiny stainless steel. The Philly Steak sandwiches were filled with thin sliced beef, tomatoes, and onions. We found Jim's version simply delicious. We ate at a counter along one wall of the cafe with a dozen other customers.

Independence Hall, cradle of liberty.

Benjamin Franklin Bridge spanning the Delaware River.

I rode out of the city over the Benjamin Franklin Bridge, across the Delaware River to Camden, New Jersey. The suspension bridge is similar in style and size to the Golden Gate and took me up five or six stories above the river. I only had the Hudson left to cross now. Camden was a more complex city than I anticipated and, very soon after descending from the bridge, I discovered I had no idea which way to turn. I found a policeman sitting in his patrol car and asked directions. He carefully explained where I was to go, when to turn, how many blocks to go before I turned and the street name I should look for. Then he said, "You know this is not a great place for a bike ride. You really shouldn't be riding around in this neighborhood. After you leave here, you don't stop, even if someone asks you to. It would be better to just ride four or five miles north, at least ride until you get out of this part of the city."

As I looked around I knew that he had given me good advice. Porches sagged, windows were boarded up, car windows were covered with plastic and some of the buildings had simply collapsed. A station wagon parked along the street had a large stereo speaker sitting on the tailgate blasting out rap music. A group of people sitting in folding chairs in the shade, turned to stare at me as I rode by. I felt like a pigeon flying past a gathering of hawks. I passed an alley and saw two people pawing through a dumpster. A block later, a wild-eyed man dressed in a rags lurched across the street, yelling at the sky. I attempted to look invulnerable and strong as I raced out of the city along River Road heading north and east.

I thought I was out of the dangerous part of the city, but when I approached an intersection and saw a car on my right, I found trouble. The car was waiting at a stop sign to pull out onto the River Road. Just before I passed in front of the car, I looked over and made eye

Above us, framed photos of celebrities covering the wall with testimonials to the quality of Jim's steak sandwiches.

After lunch, all three of us jumped on our bikes and rode up to the historical district to visit the Liberty Bell and Independence Hall. While the National Park Service guide was giving us the history of the bell, my attention began to wander away from her lesson and to refocus on the ride and the many miles I still wanted to travel before the end of the day. The journey was nearly complete and I was finding it difficult to concentrate on anything else but finishing. I said good-bye to Eric, thinking what a special week it had been. Pennsylvania had been an interesting and challenging ride. Eric's daily enthusiasm, despite the oppressive heat and humidity, had supplied the energy to get me through that heat and across the mountains at a time when my own passion for the journey was beginning to fade.

contact with the driver. He definitely saw me, but as I passed in front of him, he started moving toward me. I was going just fast enough that he missed me. I didn't like the look he gave me when we made eye contact, and I'll always believe that he actually tried to run into me. Perhaps he was only trying to scare me. He certainly succeeded. It would be the one moment during the entire trip when I felt truly threatened by a driver.

I made good time and met Nancy in Burlington about five o'clock. At this point, I had covered 40 miles for the day. We calculated that it was about twenty-five more miles to Princeton and I wanted to try and make it. She agreed to go ahead and find a place to stay. I turned east, trying to avoid some of the rush hour traffic that I thought might be heavy around Trenton a few miles to the north. I was soon riding through farmland, with fields and woods surrounding me. I was not sure, however, where I was going or exactly what road I was on. After an hour of wandering, I reached a highway and stopped to check my map. A passing cyclist saw me and shouted, "Do you need any help?" "Yes!" I hollered back. He stopped and, after some time studying my materials, sweat dripping off his forehead leaving stains on my maps, he gave me careful directions. I suppose I had ridden an extra five or six miles. Not terrible, but the bad news was that I still had a very long way to go before I reached Princeton. I called Nancy, who was having difficulties of her own with narrow roads, a large vehicle, heavy traffic and poor maps. I explained that I was running late.

It was in the high nineties all afternoon and the last few miles of my ride into Princeton were difficult. I was following Quaker Bridge Road, the same road George Washington used on January 3, 1777 to surprise the British at Princeton. This important Revolutionary War victory occurred soon after his famous Christmas night

crossing of the Delaware River at Trenton, only twelve miles away. Washington also signed the peace treaty with England in Princeton, and later gave his famous farewell-from-the-army address from the balcony of a building that has been restored and moved to the Princeton campus. The sun went down and most of the cars had their lights on by the time I arrived, shortly before 8:30, after an eighty-mile day. Nancy had found a bed and breakfast inn near the town center and the university.

We walked to a restaurant just beyond Palmer Square, the center of the village, every step an effort for me. I was tired, parched and sore. We ordered a pitcher of water and I drank most it during the meal. Even the bread, butter and salad tasted like ambrosia. I devoured every bite of my swordfish and spaghetti dinner and followed it with a chocolate sundae. I felt better, a lot better, but I still had a struggle walking the five blocks back to our room.

The Benjamin Franklin Bridge from Philadelphia to Camden, New Jersey.

Yep, the world moves pretty fast. If you don't stop and look around sometime you might miss it.

—Ferris Bueller

CHAPTER ELEVEN
New Jersey

July 29 - Day 61
Princeton to Perth Amboy
22.5 miles

After breakfast, we walked through the Princeton campus, admiring the old stone buildings, the former home of Einstein, Jodi Foster, Jimmy Stewart, Brooke Shields and Bill Bradley. The theater looked as if it had been built in the sixteenth century. The formal towers of Rockefeller College would have been right at home in Cambridge, England. It was one of most attractive campuses we had visited. I also liked that it sat directly across the street from the village center.

We returned to the room and I worked on my journal, trying to remember everything that happened during the marathon I ran the day before. At 11:30 we loaded up; Nancy drove to the laundromat and I started up Highway 27 – formerly the Lincoln Highway. The "footsteps in the sands of time" I observed while traveling the Lincoln Highway in the west, had nearly vanished here in the east, trampled and obliterated by the millions of people living here over the years. It was not difficult to imagine what driving through Princeton might have been like in the twenties, but as I headed north, there was little to remind me of a historic highway.

A few miles out of town, I worried that I might have made a wrong turn and stopped to ask two guys who were repaving an asphalt driveway for directions.

"Is this Highway 27?" I asked.

"It surely is," a stocky, very sweaty worker replied in a wonderful Irish brogue. "And where might you be headed?" I explained that I was traveling cross country from San Francisco, headed into New York City.

"Oh, golly, San Francisco! Now that's a far piece down the road. Well, it's a wonder there's not a video camera followin' you. All that way and how much weight have you lost on this trip?"

"Eight or ten pounds I think, but I'm not sure," I replied. "I haven't been near a scale for quite awhile."

"Ten pounds. I would have lost ten stone at least! How many tires did you go through? When did you start?" The conversation was a delight, a wonderful way to start my ride.

"Kingston, New Jersey," the sign said. "Settled 1675." The dates on the road signs continued to recede. It wasn't long before I was in New Brunswick, the home

A view of Rockefeller College at Princeton University.
Facing page: The New Jersey Turnpike passes under another major highway south of Elizabeth and Newark.

Monument commemorating George Washington's battle at Princeton during the Revolutionary War.

of Rutgers University. Here was a college town I wouldn't make a special trip to visit again, a sharp contrast to Princeton just fifteen miles to the south. Six or seven miles out of New Brunswick, I passed the Raritan Center, an area with three new hotels that served a large business park in the region. I called Nancy and asked her to meet me. She was only a few miles south on the New Jersey Turnpike. I secured a room at the nearest motel and then directed Nancy, by phone, right up to the front door. It was two-thirty in the afternoon and I had only traveled twenty-three miles, but this looked to be the perfect place for us to recuperate and organize ourselves for the last day, the trip to New York City.

It was strange to have nearly an entire afternoon for reading the paper and catching up on a variety of tasks the trip had forced us to put on hold. I wrote, checked our e-mail and planned my assault on Elizabeth, Newark, the George Washington Bridge and Manhattan. Nancy napped, read the paper and did some ironing while watching the news. It was a chance to recover and rest after sixteen days of constant effort.

H. Nelson Jackson and Sewell Crocker arrived in New York on July 24, 1903, sixty-three days after they left San Francisco in their two-cylinder, twenty-horsepower Winton. They became America's first transcontinental motorists. There were less than 25,000 cars in the entire country at that time. If I could find my way through the urban maze that still remained between me and the southern tip of Manhattan, I will have completed the same trip in sixty-four days. I would have to admit that the roads I traveled were significantly better that the wagon trails those pioneer motorists used.

About six o'clock, we began to think about dinner and asked the desk clerk for suggestions. Her first suggestion was Red Lobster and a list of similar franchise restaurants located along an expressway west of there.

As we started out the door, I asked a parcel delivery woman about Perth Amboy.

She wasn't very familiar with the city, but the desk clerk, who had overheard the question, said, "Do you think you might want to go into Perth Amboy?" "Yeah, it mighy be interesting," I answered, thinking that anything sounded better than a Red Lobster overlooking a local expressway.

"When you drive into Perth Amboy, you'll find Seabras Armory down on Front Street, right next to the water. It's a great spot to eat," she added.

Perth Amboy was a working class town – well cared for, with crowds moving in and out of stores along the main street, stopping to talk with their neighbors. It reminded me of those Brooklyn neighborhoods featured in the movie *Saturday Night Fever.*

Seabras Armory was indeed an experience. It featured a Spanish menu and a wonderful waiter, Jose, who had emigrated from northwest Spain in 1985. His English was broken and often difficult to understand, but his beaming friendliness more than made up for this deficiency. We sat outside under a large canopy, looking across the water to Staten Island. Families streamed by us on the boardwalk, pushing babies in strollers, making sure the older children didn't fall into the water. The soft breeze off the water was wonderful and the smell of the Atlantic signaled the end of our odyssey.

Nancy ordered the twin lobster and I had the house speciality, "Rodizia." I was served black beans, rice, greens, a fried banana and onion rings. In addition, a man would periodically stop by the table with a skewer that held roasted meat. First he arrived with pork loin and pushed a few pieces on my plate, a few minutes later beef steak showed up, then chicken, pork ribs. I lost track, but there must have been five or six different kinds of roasted meat in all.

When Jose heard from Nancy that this was the last evening of our cross-country bicycle ride, he was overcome with excitement. He wanted to find a camera to take our picture. When that didn't work, Nancy went back to the motor home to find a photocopy of the Sidney, Nebraska newspaper article. He promised to frame it and put it on the living room wall in his home. At the end of our meal we were treated to dessert (flan and chocolate mousse) and a delicious Spanish aperitif. He shook hands with both of us and we bid farewell to our new friend.

After dinner we walked out on the pier that projected into the harbor in front of the old brick armory. The bridge to Staten Island, about a mile away, soared over the water. Along the entire length of the span, lights twinkled, reflecting in the water. On the pier, people were fishing with elongated poles. Another group was trying to catch crabs using long-handled nets and flashlights. Nancy immediately began helping one group, pointing to crabs swimming near the pier, just below the surface of the water. She quickly became just another member of the crab catching team. The evening that had seemed destined to be mundane, with dinner at a Red Lobster restaurant overlooking an expressway, turned out fine – a good way to spend our last night on the trail.

Nothing compares to the simple pleasure of a bike ride.

—John F. Kennedy

CHAPTER TWELVE
New York

July 30 - Day 62
Perth Amboy to New York City
59.7 miles

I was awake for an hour at four in the morning, unable to get back to sleep, reviewing the coming day and the complex route through urban New Jersey. The events of the past two months also came to mind, the mountains, the deserts, the storms on the prairies, the heat and humidity and the people along the way. I turned over, returned to a fitful sleep, and awoke shortly before eight. It was time to finish the adventure.

We prepared well the night before and it didn't take long to load the motor home. Nancy and I checked her route along the turnpike to an RV park in Jersey City, where she would park the motor home for five days while we visited our daughter Whitney in Manhattan.

Whitney is twenty-three and works as a designer of men's knits for Federated, the parent company of Macy's and Bloomingdale's. She moved to New York City in September of 1998 after graduating from Iowa State in fashion design.

Nancy's story first. After surviving the truck lane of the New Jersey Turnpike, she parked the motor home in the RV park and then grabbed a taxi into the city. The cab's air conditioning was having difficulty reaching the back seat on this hot day, so she was invited to join her

The George Washington Bridge across the Hudson River into New York City signals the end of the journey.

The towers of Manhattan line the far shore, viewed from the center of the George Washington Bridge.

could disengage my right shoe which was clipped to my pedal, I was down, my right knee and shin skidding across the sandpaper finish of the sidewalk, leaving blood on the pavement. I ended up tumbling head over heels off the bike when my shoes released from the pedals. I jumped to my feet, feeling foolish, attempting to look as though I was totally uninjured to anyone who happened to be watching. I was lucky. I had a few scrapes and bruises, but no damage to either myself or my bike that would delay my journey.

Bill Hoffman had furnished me with my route through this northern part of the state, home to a significant amount of urban decay. I also wanted to avoid the continuous steam of eighteen-wheelers heading into and out of the city. I received an e-mail from Roger Salquist, a friend at home, predicting I would have more trouble getting through Elizabeth and Newark than I had crossing the Sierras or the Rockies. I hoped he was wrong. Bill's route was not simple. It did, however, provide me with a series of safe, connecting, suburban roads with moderate traffic, much of it through shady residential neighborhoods. The quality of those neighborhoods varied quite a bit. Newark and Hackensack, not so good; Hasbrouck Heights and Ft. Lee, nice with flower shops, sidewalk cafes and expensive foreign cars. Downtown Newark wasn't as bad as I'd feared, particularly at midday. Many fine old buildings still remained. It wasn't so wonderful that I thought I was in downtown San Francisco, but at least it wasn't scary.

I missed a few turns along the way, but there were a lot of turns and many name changes as streets passed from one town to the next. I was never off my route (I've christened it the Bill Hoffman Bike Trail) more than a block or two, but I did stop to ask directions and check my maps often. Many of the people I approached with questions had limited English and were difficult to un-

Pakistani driver in the front. Just as the two of them were exiting the Lincoln Tunnel, coming out from under the Hudson River, the driver discovered that he had lost his brakes. He still wanted to get Nancy up to 82nd Street to Whitney's apartment. I guess he thought he could stop the car by dragging his foot, but Nancy wanted out. She found a second cab and managed to arrive in the upper east side all in one piece.

I was on the road before nine and everything was going well; both the road and the traffic were fine. I rode through the town of Woodbridge. Six miles into my day, at the end of Main Street, I turned right along a curbed sidewalk and looked to my left, to see if I was going in the right direction. I wasn't. I turned back and discovered that my bike was leaning, tipping over to the right. I attempted to turn to maintain balance, but, because I was riding right up against the curb, I couldn't. Before I

derstand, but all felt inclined to point in one direction or the other, occasionally in the direction from which I had just arrived.

After about forty miles of riding, I was in Fort Lee. Finding the approach to the pedestrian path on the George Washington Bridge proved to be the most difficult navigation problem of the ride. I asked four different people for directions and the consensus of the these people had me headed onto the bridge a little early. I had been directed into the eastbound lanes, joining the trucks and cars going across the bridge. As I rode past a car stopped at a toll booth, a policeman waved me down. "Hey, where do you think you're going?" We talked for a minute and he sent me back and around to the access road that lead me to the pedestrian walkway.

The original Lincoln Highway started at Times Square and went directly west along 42nd Street to the Hudson River where ferries carried the cars to Hoboken, New Jersey. The highway continued from there to Newark, Elizabeth, Princeton and Philadelphia. I considered three options as I planned my trip into New York. The bridges to Staten Island from New Jersey did not allow cyclists, but if Nancy gave me a ride across the bridge, I could take the Staten Island Ferry and sail past the Statue of Liberty, arriving in Battery Park surrounded by the towers of lower Manhattan. The least exciting option, involved taking a PATH train from Penn Station in Newark under the Hudson to the railroad station below the 110-story World Trade Center. My choice of the George Washington Bridge was longer, but included the appeal-

ing high crossing of the Hudson River with views down the entire length of the island of Manhattan – and the perfect fantasy ending to a long cross country trip, a long ride down Broadway, New York's oldest street.

Crossing over the Hudson River, I felt the same strong emotions I had when I'd conquered the last of the mountains of the west – reaching the summit of Sherman Hill between Laramie and Cheyenne. Here, however, I was feeling more relieved than triumphant. As I crossed into my twelfth and final state, it now seemed I was going to survive this thing and actually ride down Broadway past all the many New York City landmarks. With a lump in my throat, another appropriate song came to mind.

"Give my regards to Broadway. Remember me at Herald Square. Tell all the gang at Forty-second Street, that I'll soon be there." I stopped mid-span and called "my gang at 42nd Street," Nancy and Whitney, who were having lunch together.

"I'll soon be there!" I said. I was later than I had planned, but it had been a difficult journey through the wilderness of northern New Jersey.

Riverside Drive on the west side of Manhattan was one of the best rides of the trip. The Hudson lay shimmering through the trees to my right and I was sailing down a nearly deserted road with few traffic signals. The George Washington Bridge enters the island at 178th Street and I was moving south at the rate of five streets a minute. I stopped to take a picture of Grant's Tomb and Riverside Church at 122nd Street. The church tower

Two views of Grant's Tomb on Riverside Drive. Note the bicycle pictured in the old post card.

Left: Bill approaches Times Square on Broadway.
Right: All Smiles. Bill and Nancy at Times Square, the eastern terminus of the Lincoln Highway.

prising when you consider that there are ten thousand bicycle messengers roaming the streets of New York City. Traffic slowed for lights or for delivery vans parked in the middle of the street, leaving opportunities for me and the other riders. There were split seconds to make decisions. We would squeeze through, around, and between the lines of cars. It was exciting, exhilarating, and more than a little dangerous.

At 65th Street I passed Lincoln Center and the Metropolitan Opera House. In 1966, I had spent a summer working in New York for the Benton and Bowles advertising agency. A high point of that summer occurred when I took a date for an evening at the New York Film Festival. Our taxi pulled into the same line as the limousines, and we felt like one of the arriving celebrities. I thought about waving to the crowd when we had disembarked the taxi.

At 59th, I stopped between two lanes of traffic to take a picture of Columbus Circle. Marquees for *Cats* and *Annie Get Your Gun* signaled my arrival in the theater district. At 47th, I was greeted by my small cheering section, Whitney and Nancy, who were waiting in a restaurant at the upper end of Times Square. It was nearly 2:30 and I was over an hour late, hungry and thirsty. I gave Whitney a hug and Nancy a kiss, before diving into my lunch. At 3:00, Whitney needed to get back to work at her office at 40th and Broadway, and I

rises nineteen stories into the sky, with a belfry holding a carillon of 65 bells.

At 86th Street, I moved east a block east to Broadway, that ancient trail originally followed by Indians, the island's first occupants, and began playing tag with all the Yellow Cabs. I saw more bike riders on Broadway in two blocks than I had seen during the last two months while crossing the entire country. This was not too sur-

still wanted to finish my ride down the island to Battery Park. We took several pictures in Times Square – a colorful collage of huge billboards, neon lights and tourists. When we finished, I returned to the stream of traffic moving south down Broadway.

The ride through the Garment District was next. Then Herald Square and Macy's appeared at 34th Street. I rode past Madison Square Park and the Flatiron Building at 23rd and Fifth Avenue and Union Square, with a fruit and vegetable market in full swing. Just beyond, I nearly ran into a taxi that was attempting to beat the light. I managed to stop, then pulled back out of the way and waved him through. I lectured myself to be careful. There was no need to hurry now.

Just exactly one week before I arrived in the New York, another cyclist who had also successfully ridden a Trek bicycle was welcomed with a ticker tape parade. Lance Armstrong, the American winner of the Tour d'France, certainly deserved all the honors and attention he received. It did seem a little unfair that the only notice I received in the city was from a bus driver who waved me through an intersection and a bike messenger who yelled at me to get out of his way.

The East Village flowed by and I crossed Bleecker Street. After Soho, I came to City Hall and the twin towers of the World Trade Center off to the right. Next was Wall Street and Trinity Church, the American Stock Exchange and finally Bowling Green and Battery Park at the end of the island. The park was crowded with tourists, many lined up to take the boat ride to Liberty and Ellis Islands. I found Nancy, armed with her video camera, recording the end of our adventure.

Two tasks remained to be completed. I pulled the small bottle of Pacific Ocean water, that I had carried

The ride down Broadway.
Left to right:
The Flatiron Building,
City Hall,
Trinity Church,
and Bowling Green.

Left: Bill attempts to dip his wheel in New York Harbor.
Right: A bottle of water from the Pacific Ocean is poured into the harbor, the Statue of Liberty in the distance.

for over 3,300 miles, out of my bike bag and poured it into the harbor while Nancy recorded it with her cameras, the Statue of Liberty in the distance.

My last official act was to dip the front wheel of my bike into the harbor. I started toward the water and discovered a rather serious problem. The water was over eight feet below the level of the ground I was standing on and was separated from the park by a fence and a stone sea wall. I removed everything I could from my bike, lifted it over the fence and climbed over after it, wheeling it down a ramp toward the water. Then I kneeled down on the slippery, moss-covered, wooden bumper that acted as a cushion for the Liberty Island ferry when it docked. I kneeled on the bumper, holding onto my rear wheel, reaching down, dangling my bike over the side. My front wheel was just able to touch the surface of the water. I managed the whole episode with-

out either dropping the bike or slipping off my narrow ledge. I wasn't sure I would make the *New York Times* if I fell into the harbor; but, if I required a special rescue effort, with several emergency vehicles, after a cross-country bike ride, I just might.

I returned to the safety of the park. Nancy had an appointment with Whitney's hairdresser and I still needed to ride up to Whitney's apartment on East 82nd. We congratulated each other, exchanged a kiss and big hug and parted ways. I rode past the Staten Island Ferry terminal, the South Street Seaport and the Fulton Fish Market, before stopping to have a passing businessman take a picture of me with the Brooklyn Bridge in the background.

New York had the hottest July in recorded history. The rest of the East Coast was also setting records and it had been hot again in the afternoon, over ninety degrees. I was tired, relieved and satisfied when I arrived, around 5:30, at Whitney's apartment and rolled my bike into the elevator. I'd enjoyed riding in the city and thought I might want to try a little more before we left. After two flat tires in one day near Tama, Iowa, I had crossed all or part of seven other states without incident. Go figure. I had ridden for nineteen straight days to conclude the trip. I was unsure what this odyssey might mean to me eventually. I needed a chance to recover and think about it. Maybe, in a few days, I'd have an idea or two. Right then, just getting off my bike was enough.

Captain Joshua Slocum was the first man to sail alone around the world. These are the last words he wrote in his journal at the conclusion of the voyage in 1898:

"And now, without having wearied my friends, I hope, with detailed scientific accounts, theories, or deductions, I will only say that I have endeavored to tell just the story of the adventure itself. This, in my own poor way, having been done, I now moor ship, weather-bitt cables, and leave the sloop Spray, for present, safe in port."

My ship was safe in port. The "story of the adventure itself" was finished.

Views of lower Manhattan from the Brooklyn Bridge, and Bill at the end of the journey.

For my part,
I travel not to go anywhere, but to go.
I travel for travel's sake.
The great affair is to move.

—Robert Louis Stevenson

EPILOGUE

Back home, I remembered the wonderful simplicity of each day on the road. I missed that. I knew exactly what I needed to accomplish – the number of miles to ride, the town to reach before nightfall. Success was easily measured, if not easily accomplished. Life was simple – reach the goal and feel good. I felt good, day after day.

I also miss the adventure, the fact that on any given day I really didn't know what was going to happen, what surprise would be around the next bend in the road. There was a sense of magical possibility – that literally anything could happen. When you're young, the world is an exciting place, primarily because you've experienced so little of it. Everything is new – each day a voyage of discovery. No matter how well our lives have turned out as we grow older, we miss that. We know what will happen next and next ... and how the journey will end. This trip was a gift, a chance to rediscover the excitement, adventure and innocence of my youth, if only for a few weeks.

In the beginning of the trip, the ability to eat virtually anything was terrific. Milkshakes, which had become a rare treat in the last decade, were suddenly available on a daily basis. They tasted marvelous, especially when made the old fashioned way, with real ice cream and lots of chocolate sauce, like the one I had at Ditto's Cafe in Stanwood, Iowa. Eating and talking with people while sitting at counters and around tables in small town diners along our route were wonderful ways to feel the pulse of this country – to learn about its character.

So, there were advantages – simplicity, adventure

A "welcome home" sign on the garage door as Nancy starts unloading the motor home.

and lots to eat – but riding a bike across the country was not a pleasure cruise. It would have been more fun in '57 Chevy convertible. For me, the trip was a test to see if I could still succeed at a task that was primarily physical. Maybe a bit of a mid-life crisis, definitely a learning experience. I was surprised by what I could ask my body to accomplish, even when I was exhausted. I was also surprised, that after an evening when I was too tired to walk across the street, I could recover sufficiently to resume my journey in the morning.

Following the Lincoln Highway turned out to be an excellent choice. It seemed to pull the days together like beads on a string. It connected us to the generations of people who previously traveled along these historic routes. We compared our trip with the journeys that those early travelers made over the same ground. We were moving across the country with ghosts – the pony express riders, the pioneers who rode in the wagon trains, the builders of the transcontinental railroad, and the early Lincoln Highway motorists. We sought evidence of their passing and enjoyed every discovery that confirmed their existence. I became a highway historian, an archeologist on a bicycle.

Security is mostly a superstition. It does not exist in nature nor do the children of men experience it as a whole. Avoiding danger is no safer in the long run than outright exposure. Life is either a daring adventure or it is nothing.
—Helen Keller

When I came across this quote at my sister's house in Chicago, I was surprised. I read it again. Surely it must be important to avoid danger, to use common sense. But the more I thought about what this blind, deaf, remarkable woman had said, the more I liked it. Life is for living, for seeking daring adventure. We need to avoid the complacency that surrounds our lives, suffocating them with comfort and routine. She was right. We aren't any safer when we hide from danger. Injuries and disease are not strangers in our homes. John Glenn, the 1962 *Mercury* astronaut, returned to space at seventy-seven years of age and said, "Nothing is one hundred percent risk free – nothing. But the gain to be made is worth that risk." If we never escape the security of our ordinary rational lives, we will certainly miss out on those magical possibilities, the chance that almost anything might happen.

When our journey was finished, I wasn't sure I would ever consider another bike trip, but I must admit that I have caught the fever. Just the idea of another journey is the perfect antidote for the many everyday concerns that often become too important. The west coast of California would be a beautiful trip and I've always wanted to explore the length of Route 66. Why not on a bike?

ACKNOWLEDGEMENT

There are many people I would like to recognize who provided generous assistance. Sharon Todd, the bicycle coordinator from the state of Ohio, sent me twenty-five photocopied pages of maps marked with colored pens, indicating potential routes across her entire state. Thanks for guiding me away from the dangerous highways to your quiet back roads. Adventure Cycling publishes *The Cyclists' Yellow Pages* that is an invaluable guide for the cross-country biker. I found the phone numbers for all twelve State Bicycle Coordinators I spoke with, and to other resources I used planning my trip.

Lincoln Highway Association members Greg Franzwa and Jess Petersen offered advice and guide books to sections of the highway for Utah, Wyoming, Nebraska and Iowa. Mike Buettner provided Lincoln Highway information for Indiana and Ohio. He also marked up a set of maps guiding me to the best routes across this section of the country with notes highlighting the points of interest I would be riding by. Mike also published excerpts from my journal in the Ohio Lincoln Highway Newsletter. Also, thanks to Joe Schlechter from Davis who provided me with historical materials for California.

I am especially grateful to Bill Hoffman who answered my desperate plea for help to the Lancaster Bicycle Club. I was hoping for advice on riding into and through Philadelphia. Bill initially providing me with routes from Pittsburgh to Philadelphia. Ultimately, he gave me the important advice that guided me through the urban maze of northern New Jersey across the Hudson into New York City.

Bob Brouhard, my neighbor, inspired me with his many cycling exploits, advised me on equipment and training, and called me several times to check on my progress across the country. Thanks to Jeff Hein at Freewheeler in Davis for his quick lessons on changing a spoke and fixing a chain and for preparing my bike so well I didn't need to use either of them. Chuck Kolbe convinced me to ride across Iowa with him in 1997 and showed me how much fun cross-country cycling could be. He also taught me that speed was one of the least important objectives on a cross-country ride.

Many thanks to the friends and family that followed our voyage via e-mail and telephone – sharing our pain and our excitement. Your generous support and encouragement raised our spirits and made Nancy and I feel like we had never left home. A special thanks to the Stilles in Reno, the Kolbes in Des Moines, the Kaspereks in Hinsdale and Bill Hoffman in Lancaster. Your hospitality gave us a chance to rest, recover and get off the road for a night.

Particular thanks to my riding companions, Mike Thieroff and Eric Roe, who pedaled with me through some difficult miles of mountains in Nevada and Pennsylvania. My only regret is that we were unable to share more of the journey together. A special thank you to Whitney Roe who helped celebrate my arrival at Times Square and hosted us for a week in her studio apartment.

I am grateful to Duane and Jeanette Copley who read an early draft of my journal. They diplomatically called errors to my attention while encouraging my efforts. I want to thank my editor, Kelly Wilkerson, for her lessons in language and style, and her belief in the project. Her blue pencil helped shape the journal and curbed some of my enthusiasm for describing, among other things, everything I ate during the day. My neighbor, Sally Hosley, read the final manuscript, fine tuning my text while providing positive advice and suggestions. She also introduced me to the publishing and distribution world.

Above all, I want to thank and recognize my colleague and collaborator, Alison Roe. She read the journal, created the title and designed the book. Her attention to detail is evident on every page. She became the person that listened to my concerns, offered encouragement and suggestions, and made the final product look better than I ever believed possible. Our shared efforts became a second journey that was in many ways as memorable and exciting as the first.

DAY	DATE	CITY	MILES/DAY	TOTAL MILES	DAY	DATE	CITY	MILES/DAY	TOTAL MILES
1	26 May	San Francisco, CA	Start Trip	0.00	32	30 June	Columbus	70.56	1,723.23
2	27 May	Davis	74.58	74.58	33	1 July	Missouri Valley, IA	88.59	1,811.82
3	28 May	Loomis	65.17	139.75	34	2 July	Westside	74.97	1,886.79
4	29 May	Baxter	46.75	186.49	35	3 July	Boone	70.56	1,957.35
5	30 May	Truckee	39.10	225.60	36	4 July	Des Moines	Rest Day	
6	4 June	Reno, NV	30.18	255.78	37	5 July	Marshalltown	61.64	2,019.00
7	5 June	Fallon	64.68	320.46	38	6 July	Cedar Rapids	73.30	2,092.30
8	6 June	Middlegate	53.41	373.87	39	7 July	Clinton	85.95	2,178.25
9	7 June	Austin	65.17	439.04	40	8 July	Rochelle, IL	72.03	2,250.28
10	8 June	Eureka	70.76	509.80	41	9 July	Aurora	50.86	2,301.14
11	9 June	Ely	79.38	589.18	42	10 July	Hinsdale	Rest Day	
12	10 June	Leges Station	57.53	646.70	43	11 July	Hinsdale	Rest Day	
13	11 June	Wendover	59.78	706.48	44	12 July	Deep River, IN	73.70	2,374.83
14	12 June	Tooele, UT	77.13	783.61	45	13 July	Plymouth	59.49	2,434.32
15	13 June	Salt Lake	49.29	832.90	46	14 July	Columbia City	42.43	2,476.75
16	14 June	Salt Lake	Rest Day		47	15 July	Van Wert, OH	63.70	2,540.45
17	15 June	Coalville	46.55	879.45	48	16 July	Lima	39.10	2,579.56
18	16 June	Evanston, WY	41.75	921.20	49	17 July	Upper Sandusky	51.74	2,631.30
19	17 June	Lyman	44.69	965.89	50	18 July	Jeromesville	53.80	2,685.10
20	18 June	Rock Springs	58.70	1,024.59	51	19 July	East Rochester	63.70	2,748.80
21	19 June	Wamsutter	65.66	1,090.25	52	20 July	Beaver, PA	52.43	2,801.23
22	20 June	Rawlins	56.55	1,146.80	53	21 July	Irwin	53.12	2,854.35
23	21 June	Laramie	83.10	1,229.90	54	22 July	Somerset	54.39	2,908.74
24	22 June	Laramie	Rest Day		55	23 July	Breezewood	55.37	2,964.11
25	23 June	Cheyenne	58.70	1,288.60	56	24 July	Chambersburg	52.53	3,016.64
26	24 June	Kimball, NB	64.78	1,353.38	57	25 July	York	52.63	3,069.26
27	25 June	Sidney	38.81	1,392.19	58	26 July	Lancaster	23.81	3,093.08
28	26 June	Ogallala	68.31	1,460.49	59	27 July	Paoli	55.37	3,148.45
29	27 June	North Platte	50.86	1,511.36	60	28 July	Princeton, NJ	80.65	3,229.10
30	28 June	Lexington	65.17	1,576.53	61	29 July	Perth Amboy	22.54	3,251.64
31	29 June	Grand Island	76.15	1,652.67	62	30 July	New York, NY	59.68	3,311.32

We all possess a predilection for lostness,
some of us more than others.
But lostness, like all talents, must be nurtured,
developed and practiced in order to enjoy its benefits.
Many of my friends know where they have been, where
they are and where they are headed.
How sad.

—Marla Streb

BIBLIOGRAPHY

Ambrose, Stephen E. *Undaunted Courage: Meriwether Lewis, Thomas Jefferson, and the Opening of the American West.* New York: Simon & Schuster, 1996.

Butko, Brian A. *A Pennsylvania Traveler's Guide to the Lincoln Highway.* Mechanicsburg, PA: Stackpole, 1996.

Dodge, Pryor. Introduction by David V. Herlihy *The Bicycle.* Paris-New York: Flammarion, 1996.

Franzwa, Gregory M. *The Lincoln Highway: Iowa: Volume 1, Nebraska:Volume 2 and Wyoming: Volume 3.* Tucson, AZ: The Patrice Press, 1995, 1996, 1999.

Hokanson, Drake. *The Lincoln Highway: Main Street Across America.* Iowa City: University of Iowa Press, 1988.

Ikenberry, Donna Lynn. *Bicycling Coast to Coast: A Complete Route Guide Virginia to Oregon.* Seattle, WA: The Mountaineers, 1996.

Jenkins, Peter. *A Walk Across America.* New York: William Morrow & Company, Inc., 1979.

Kauffman, Richard. Text from John Muir. *Gentle Wilderness: The Sierra Nevada.* New York: Promontory Press, 1967.

Kropp, Göran, David Lagercrantz. *Ultimate High: My Everest Odyssey.* New York: Discovery Books, 1997.

Kurmaskie, Joe. *Metal Cowboy: Tales From the Road Less Pedaled.* New York: Breakaway Books, 1999.

Lamb, David. *Over the Hills: A Midlife Escape Across America by Bicycle.* New York: Random House, 1996.

Loher, George T. *The Wonderful Ride: Being the True Journal of Mr. George T. Loher Who in 1895 Cycled from Coast to Coast on his Yellow Fellow Wheel.* San Francisco: Harper & Row, Publishers, 1978.

Newhouse, Brian. *A Crossing: A Cyclist's Journey Home.* New York: Pocket Books, 1998.

Protteau, Lyn. *The Lincoln Highway: The Story of a Crusade That Made Transportation History.* New York: Dodd, Mead, 1935

Slocum, Captain Joshua. *Sailing Alone Around the World.* New York: Dover Publications, 1956.

Utley, Robert M. *A Life Wild and Perilous: Mountain Men and the Paths to the Pacific.* New York: Henry Holt and Company, 1997.

Wallis, Michael. *Route 66: The Mother Road.* New York: St. Martin's Press, 1990.

Weir, Willie. *Spokesongs: Bicycle Adventures on Three Continents.* Seattle, WA: Pineleaf Productions, 1997.

Journeys, like artists,
are born and not made.
A thousand differing circumstances
contribute to them,
few of them willed
or determined by will
 — whatever we may think.
They flower spontaneously
out of the demands of our natures
 — and the best of them lead us
not only outwards in space,
but inwards as well.
Travel can be one of the most
rewarding forms of introspection ...

—Lawrence Durrell